spanish folk crafts

spanish folk crafts

Mª antonia pelauzy

photographer

f. català roca

editorial blume

milanesado 21-23   barcelona 17

"NUEVA IMAGEN" Series

First published 1978
Translated from the Spanish by Diorki

ISBN 84-7031-060-7
Library of Congress Catalog Card Number: 77-93979

© 1978 by Editorial Blume, Barcelona
Dep. legal B. 7531-1978
Printed in Spain by Emograph, S.A., Almirante
Oquendo, 1, Barcelona

Manufactured in Spain

contents

introduction

Everywhere today there is a firm and growing interest in folk art and traditional crafts, not as archaic objects on display in well-tended museums, but as something still alive which we must discover and appreciate before it is too late. For the extinction of this world goes hand in hand with the disappearance of traditional ways of life, some of them a thousand years old: the great exodus from the country to the city and mass communication media, especially television, homogenize customs, fill everyone's free time with the same entertainment, wiping out old customs and weakening beliefs.

This gradual process has occurred throughout Europe, and in a few countries there remain—in a slow and sometimes painful process of extinction—rural communities with sufficient vitality and self-sufficiency to continue producing all the goods needed for their ancestral activities; also dying out are the small, family workshops where articles were handcrafted, not so much for household use as for use in farm production; and even the small factories which had been somewhat mechanized are disappearing under the pressure of new kinds of demand and economic rules of production.

In this commentary, we include, but wish to distinguish between, the folk arts and handcrafts of rural production and those of urban production, such as some kinds of carpentry-cabinet-making, bone-lace work, religious images, toys, which are the work of small local artisans with family workshops, whose products are for a wider market than the strictly rural, and are more often decorative than utilitarian. We include this type of production because, with greater or less perfection and refinement, they are an ingenuous, less elaborate version of the "luxury" arts: a "folk" version that has been adopted by the people.

The purpose of this book is to offer, through the striking and human photographs of Catalá Roca, a vision of this world which is escaping from us, bowing before the impetus of new life styles. In a few years nothing will remain of this whole world of archaic forms we see in the countryside of the Iberian Peninsula—large, narrow-mouthed jugs, shepherds' cabins, baskets for gathering harvests—nor of the ingenuous figures for Nativity scenes made and sold in some Spanish cities, of the forms of bread baked in neigh-borhood bakeries, or the incredible frameworks for fireworks displays. Time counts too heavily today for

these objects to endure—these objects which mark a different rhythm than the rhythms that rule in the world of planning, of great markets, and of mass production to supply them. Folk arts and handicrafts have never been produced in a hurry; even the most elementary forms evolved over many years, and in each article we find the mark of the intimate detail of the artisan's finishing touches, his own fondness for the object which makes each piece unique. Not even pieces of pottery, which seem the crude work of the potter's wheel, are missing the imprint; the potter has taken them in his hands so often... forming the object, letting it dry, adding the handle when it is soft... letting it dry again, polishing it, putting it in the kiln and then taking it out. Yet it is a humble object, made along with many others, sold unpretentiously, bought in a market to be used. And there lies our discovery when we are struck by the power of its "design", the elementary way it was made, its artlessness and simplicity. On this adventure of discovery we have set out in this work, which does not pretend to be learned, but empathetic, a kind of itinerary through materials, ways of working with them, and objects that still have their reason for being, either in daily use, or fulfilling the social function of adornment, gift, or entertainment. Some manifestations may be something as simple as the barns for storing hay that dot the landscape, or the way of tying up sheaves—these too must be caught and appreciated for they will soon disappear from view. Other times it will be the familiar sight of the *botijo,* the earthenware jug with an opening for pouring in water and a spout for drinking, so perfectly adapted to its function that it is an example of pre-industrial "design". And still other times it is the primordial need for ornamentation and occupation epitomized by the shepherd's carving knife.

This panorama takes in all Spain, and we shall speak, then, of folk arts in Spain, for there is no single thing we can call Spanish folk art. Folk art has common roots, and if similar manifestations appear in distant places, it is because the origin is very basic, felt in the same way, and similar solutions may be found in different communities. Within the political unit that is Spain, there are geographic and historical elements that produce a rich diversity. Spain has been a bridge between Europe and Africa. Over the years, various peoples and cultures have co-existed and been superimposed, one over the other, on the peninsula: Celts, Iberians, Greeks, Carthaginians, Romans, Visigoths, and Arabs. And the profound experience later on with the New World contributed too to the peculiar configuration of the various communities that make up the whole of Spain. Moreover, for many centuries, Spain has exported to Europe handcrafted products of oriental origin: leather work, glazed ceramics of Arab origin, the damascened iron and steel of Toledo. And although these products may have lost their importance in the world of "luxury arts", there are still the know-how, the traditions of certain crafts that have humbly found acceptance in a wider, less refined field. A difficult geography, with a ring of several mountain ranges, and climate variations from arid, African areas to the rainy regions of the north, have given rise to very varied ways of life and so to different ways of satisfying elementary needs; and, while the peninsula remains open to all kinds of influences, it has perpetuated archaic forms and models. So we find everything from articles harking back to Iberian or Roman culture—such as the earthenware of Priego (in the province of Cuenca) or Llamas de Mouro (in Asturias), or the Roman plow still used in many fields, to the charming Nativity scene figures of Murcia which have their origin in the Nativity scenes of baroque Naples, or the slender or baroque palm branches fashioned for Palm Sunday. We give thanks to all those artisans who have shown us their crafts and have let themselves be photographed at their work, work which they believe to be a symbol of underdevelopment, and in which they continue to engage, almost apologetically, as their only way of making a living. They are not aware of the beauty of their work, for this is not their motivation, nor of the traditional content they have mastered. We, in search of this knowledge which has no historical date, but is linked to something past, try to recover some of these objects, but not, as Octavio Paz says, to make of them unique objects as works of art, but as samples of many: "The work of the artisan escapes from the museum, and when it falls into one, it holds its own with honor: it is not unique, it is an example. It is a captive sample, not an idol."

textile arts

weaving

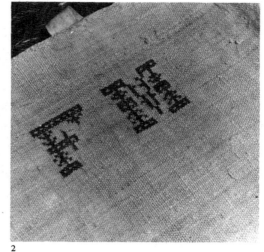

1   Antique woolen apron with silk trim and embroidery

2   Linen apron, used in butchering pigs, with cross-stitched initials. Balearic Islands

3   Delicate "gorullo" coverlet from a family loom in Galicia

Spain has had rich and long-standing traditions in textiles throughout its history. The cultivation of flax and the use of the silkworm, together with the quality of the wool, gave rise to important textile industries in all of Muslim Spain, since the Arabs, who imported textile techniques and designs unknown in Medieval Europe, gave the impetus for the creation of workshops in Málaga, Almería, Granada and Valencia, as well as in Sicily. In these cities, beautiful and refined silks and linens and lovely carpets were produced. This industry began to decline gradually after the expulsion of the Moors, and finally disappeared altogether in the early decades of the nineteenth century. This whole world of luxurious and costly fabrics reached into the lower classes: while they did not use them, they did learn the techniques and adopted the Moorish designs, with simplifications and deformations, in the making of textiles for their own use. Thus we find well into the nineteenth century beautiful embroidery with oriental designs, coverlets in "comfit" weave, "loom net", and the fabrics and rugs of the Alpujarra region, which show us how traditional Arabic fabrics and embroideries have been conserved throughout the slow evolution of the society. We can consider them a genuine expression of national popular taste through the centuries.

There are still living examples of this rich tradition and it is urgent that we learn about them, as month by month they grow scarcer or more decadent. Economic conditions and geographical characteristics have enabled artisan activities which have disappeared in other European countries to endure in Spain; and in spite of the great development of the cotton industry in Catalonia, there were, in the early decades of this century, many villages

3

where the women spun, wove, and embroidered linens and outer wear for family use. Remember that in the mountains, where there is an exclusively agrarian economy and villages are widely scattered, we still find the village self-sufficiency of centuries ago. The first thing to disappear, although aprons, towels, and sheets can still be found yet unused among the possessions of fifty- or sixty-year old village women, was homespun linen—plain cloth in which warp and woof are of flax; it has been replaced by cotton woven in factories and sold at low prices. The cultivation of flax, which needs fertile land and careful irrigating, has given way to other crops, and we have found fields of flax only in occasional villages in Galicia, Extremadura, and the Canary Islands. And so, in other fabrics which used a warp of flax, this fiber has been replaced by industrial cotton. Another factor we should bear in mind in order to understand the rapid impoverishment of domestic weaving, not only of flax but also of wool, is the massive emigration from the poorest rural areas to the cities, decimating villages and destroying the ties of the rural family to the land, its crops, its traditions and its continuity. We have found a pathetic example among Galician village women who keep their loom set up with a coverlet started on it; but they scarcely work at it since the daughters for whom the coverlet is intended are far away, in a big city or in a foreign country, and they don't expect to return to the traditional ways of life.

Woolen fabrics for outdoor use (saddle-bags, horse blankets, or shepherds' blankets), in greater demand, could be made on the family loom, or ordered from weaving families who had several looms which were worked by members

5

consumption—domestic, exclusively for family use; that of family workshops, either made to order or sold in local markets; and that of small industries that supply a wider market, or which sell their wares as ornamental rather than utilitarian articles—we shall try to describe the principal techniques used in each of them.

Plain Fabric
In this kind of weaving, using warp and woof of flax, and an unvarying motion of the shuttle, heavy cloth was made for embroidering hand towels, aprons, and sheets, in spite of the fabric's being unquestionably rough and stiff. This cloth comes from family looms made, as are animal carts, by skilled rural carpenters or by a member of the family itself. Majorca and Minorca produced this type of linen until very recently, and used it especially for aprons for the annual event of butchering the pig; there are still many of them in use, as they are most durable. In Fuentearcada, a village near Ginzo de Limia (in the province of Orense), there was a household loom still being used to weave linen for sheets in 1974, and another in Fonte-Chantada (Lugo).

Plain woolen fabrics and cloth made with warp of cotton and woof of wool are used for coverlets, blankets, saddle-bags, and decorative cloths. By plain fabric, we mean one with no textured design, since the shuttle always follows the same movement among the strands of the warp; it may, however, have several colors, or form regular squares, by playing woof against warp.

We have seen that these fabrics are still being made on many household looms in the province of Albacete, in **Bogarra, Alcadozo, Tobarra**, and **El Bonillo**, among others, for local use, as they are used to cover the wide benches found in all the houses in the village, and for

4   Beautiful fabrics are found in the homes of all Galician villages

5   Coarse saddle-bags of white wool, with initials, made on a household loom

of the family. Raw materials were provided either by the weaving family or by the person placing the specific order. In some of these villages, the weaving families still function, or have given rise to small artisan textile industries which supply a small area with blankets and saddle-bags. Many of these small textile factories have been devoured by the competition from industrial products, or have suffered from lessening demand, a result of the movement of the rural population to the cities, as mentioned above.

Keeping in mind that there are three types of textile production and

7

8

decorative cloths and aprons; in some villages, such as El Bonillo, the tradition of dyeing still exists, so that the traditional color shadings and tones have been preserved.

There are also household looms in Zamora, used for making saddle-bags and plain woven blankets, with the classic green, red, and black of the *"sayaguesa"* blanket, named after the village of **Almeida de Sayago,** where it is found, as well as in **Torregamones** and **Moralina.** In this last village, the original loom has given way to a small industry using mechanical looms, while absorbing the isolated production of other weavers of large sacks and saddle-bags, since greater organization and production allow products to be sold in local markets of the region. The weaver of Las Torres de Aliste, who used to weave the blanket called *"alistana",* after the village, as well as large sacks and saddle-bags, moved to Madrid in 1976. That same year, the loom in Pedrazales, near Sanabria, was taken down. In these areas, there are many looms still set up but not in use, since the fabrics made on them are very costly compared to those made industrially.

Also, in the Alpujarra area of the province of Granada—in **Válor** and

Mecina Bombarón—we still find production of plain cloths, used as blankets, with the characteristic colors of the region: bands of red, black, blue and cinnamon which also appear in the famous Alpujarra rugs, but these are disappearing as the area becomes gradually and, it would appear, relentlessly, poorer and less populous. The present blankets are made with poor quality dyed wool and with scraps of old blankets or sweaters. The famous Alpujarra fabrics—coverlets of thick, loose wool which now bear the name of the region where they were mostly made—are made only in **Ugíjar,** in a subsidized shop which has introduced some novelties of doubtful judgment, and in some workshops in **Granada,** tourist-oriented, but worthy.

In the mountains of Cádiz, in **Grazalema,** there is a traditional workshop which has been newly active in recent years and continues making plain, fine, woolen fabric in white and brown for use in monastic habits but which can also serve many decorative uses. We will describe the making of the Grazalema blankets in another section along with that of several other blankets still being made locally using the old systems.

And last, we shall mention Galicia,

fabulous world of textiles, where the mother of every family had her loom, and where it seems that the old proverb, "Take a house with a hearth and a wife who can spin", is still heeded. In contrast with the women's somber dress, and the near absence of ornamental embroidery, the home-woven cloths have always shown a great wealth of skill. The looms we have seen are frequently installed in unlikely places, on the ground floor of stone houses along with farming tools and baskets, and sometimes in the the same place that serves as chicken-roost by night. From these rudimentary looms, which seem like ancient carts, have come the handsome "comfit" coverlets—thus called because of their designs which look like comfits and whose technique and origin we will mention later—, coverlets of plain fabric and, last, the simplest and most humble fabric, the blankets called *"retaleras"* or *"farrapas"* (meaning they are made from remnants or scraps), which in Galicia have delicate tones and are so beautifully made they make one forget that they are an expression of poverty. All of these articles have always been made for use in the home, and there used to be so many looms that, until a few

15

years ago, the professional weaver, making to order, did not exist. In this warm, matriarchal world of the Galician family, broken by constant emigration, all kinds of fabrics are still woven, and flax and wool are still spun very often. When the fabric is plain and of a solid color, it usually receives an embroidered design and is used as a coverlet. The strips of heavy fabric are joined together with blue thread, which is decorative in itself, and the edges are trimmed with fringe or crocheted strips. The embroidery is simple and uses floral themes.

We will mention only places where there are numerous household looms in operation and which are easy to find; otherwise, we might unwittingly send interested readers to very remote villages where, month after month, looms are left idle, and, at worst, these antique artifacts are broken up for firewood. We mention the area of Viana del Bollo—with **San Martín** and **Prada**; **Verín**, and **La Puebla de Trives**, in Orense; and **Fonsagrada**, Otero del Rey—**Robra, Begonte,** and **Donalbay**—and Chantada—**Rodeiro** and **Lalín**; in Lugo are areas where the loom is still worked.

In all of the villages, the traveler may be shown the precious coverlets, stored away in chests, part of treasured family possessions.

9   *This loom will produce a spotless white* "farrapa"

10   *The Galician family looms are kept alongside grain storage and chicken roosts*

9

16

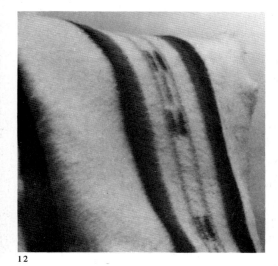

12

Blankets

These are also of a plain weave, but we are discussing them separately because of the nature of today's production and market.

Blankets of **Val de San Lorenzo** (León). These were the traditional blankets, woven of thick wool, sold in nearby markets and fairs in Lucillo, Cacabelos, and La Bañeza. In the last century there were several hand looms on which they were made, and they had an eager market. At present, almost all the looms have been mechanized, and there is a small factory which supplies colored wool and the warp thread and which sells to businesses in León and Castile. There is still one old loom worked by two women, Dolores Fernández and her mother, Carolina; a loom of this type must be worked by two people, as it is more than two meters wide and someone has to recover the shuttle from the other side. The blankets of Val are white with pink and green stripes at the ends and when they are made to order, the client's initials are included in pink. The Fernández family spins the white wool for the woof and buys the rest of the wool and the warp from the factory in the town, which spins wool from the province of Palencia. After weaving, the fabric is usually fulled, so that it tightens and shrinks, and then the pile is brushed up using thistles from Corella, in Navarre, as not all kinds of thistles will do the trick. These blankets must be handled delicately because of their coloring, and they have always been used under coverlets, as they are not considered ornamental.

Near Val, in **San Justo de la Vega**, the blankets typical of the Maragatería (region of León) are made on hand looms, of red and green. The loom is only half a meter wide, and pieces are not sewn together, so they are small and used as bedside rugs.

The blankets made in **Grazalema** (Cádiz) are exceptionally wide: there are two hand looms, three meters long, in operation which, worked by two men, produce pieces 2.40 meters wide. These pieces, made with wool spun in the same factory, from the mountains of Cádiz, are fulled for four hours, shrinking to 190 cm., and they are not brushed. These blankets preserve the traditional designs, with parallel or perpendicular strips in natural white and brown, or with some strips in blue, and are trimmed with fringe from the warp. Beginning in the last century they were sold at September fairs and were known over a wide area; then sales and production fell off to the point that the closing of the "Nuestra Señora del Carmen" factory seemed inevitable, until two young men from Arcos de la Frontera, where there were also looms, decided to revive production and save a small local industry, seeking new markets and revaluing the dignified and lovely production of Grazalema. This is a laudable and worthy effort which brings a ray of hope into the confusion that reigns in the "pious" and mistaken directions usually taken by government agencies and by private owners themselves, in the business of folk arts and crafts.

Blankets of **Ezcaray**. This textile-producing village in the province of Logroño is one of the oldest in the country, and its production is very well known. There are several old looms on which the traditional blankets of large brown and white squares are made. The spinning is also done here, since the wool used is from the district. Recently, they have made innovations in the traditional, austere designs, with colors and long fringe, thus broadening the market, but marking the tendency to adulterate traditional production.

The blankets of **Pont de Suert** (Lérida) are now woven mechanically, as the factory has been completely

11   Coverlet with simple embroidery and fringe as decoration

12   The classic blanket of fulled wool, of Val de San Lorenzo, León

13

14

15

industrialized, and they are of no interest, as they have also failed to preserve the traditional coloring.
"Rainbow" blankets. These blankets are made in Berja (Almería) and are a derivation of the cloths or coverlets made with a flax warp and loose wool woof, typical of the Alpujarra area. Here they have abandoned the classic dense, dark colors, and taken on lively, bright colors. They are made on hand looms with dyed wool of industrial origin.
The familiar and lovely blankets of Zamora, with their wide strips of red, green and white, and black or brown in the middle, have disappeared; the efforts made in Almeida de Sayago cannot be considered successful, since they use industrially spun dyed wool, and instead of being fulled, the blankets are submitted to a mechanical process which destroys their value.

"Comfit" weaves and figured cloths
There are several types of weaves other than plain. These can be classified into general categories on the basis of the techniques as follows: "comfit" weaves, *"gorullo"* weaves (a *"gorullo"* is a small button or ball of wool), and shell-work; the "net of Valdeverdeja"

13   *Blankets drying after being fulled. Grazalema, Cádiz*

14   *Fragment of a blanket*

15   *The magnificent loom of Grazalema, Cádiz*

16   *Festive horse blanket, with beautiful fringe and woven initials. Níjar, Almería*

20

16

or loom net, which we shall mention later, and figured weaves.

Comfit cloth also appears in Sicily, with some variations in design and color, and its origin is oriental. It is widespread in Spain, from Galicia to La Mancha, and is used for making coverlets. The technique can be described as a series of small, hard loops, like knots, which are achieved by loading the shuttle with a thick, twisted strand which is brought out at intervals to form the loop or "comfit", and the weaving is continued by bringing another shuttle with a fine, smooth warp thread back and forth several

times. There are comfit weavers in **Bogarra, Munera,** and **Casas de Lázaro** (Albacete). In Galicia, in the places cited above as having looms in use, they also make comfit cloth, as it is a technique often used in making coverlets for family use, with older and more schematic designs than those made in La Mancha, and therefore with a special charm, and with a tendency to make groupings of the loops, giving the effect of little flowers. All of these coverlets usually have a border of fringe. There is also a variation which consists of producing the loops with a group of loose threads, which, when short, make

a thick, soft cloth. Other times, the loops were left long and later cut, different from the English coverlets of similar technique, in which the loops formed part of the woof.

The comfit technique has been lost in many areas, such as Majorca and Catalonia, where it was used for ornamental trimming of skirts.

The open weave called loom net or net of Valdeverdeja, which has been lost completely, seems to have been a specialty of the village in the province of Toledo whose name it bears. Its technique is quite curious and permits development of very effective designs.

The shuttle never advances much, and when it arrives at the point where the open work is to begin, it is moved back, making an opening between the warp threads, to return again, as in darning. It is done on the width of the loom, and was used to make altar cloths; it was done only in white linen.

Figured weaves have been used for coverlets, for festive saddle-bags, cloths to cover furniture, and for the aprons of village dress. The design can be varied, as there is an infinite play of color and texture. Textures may be achieved by passing the thick woof at different intervals between the strands of the warp, which is thus always covered, allowing designs and textures to be made with the different thicknesses. Another type of figured weave, of simple and striking design, consists in not covering the strands of the warp, but in playing them with the same value as the woof, making a positive-negative ornamental design; thus we find many woolen saddle-bags, made in Zamora, Salamanca, and Albacete, with herringbone weaves, squares or diamonds, in only two colors. Some coverlets have been made with this technique just about everywhere, but we have found some made approximately between 1950 and 1960 in **Morella** (Castellón), **Almeida de Sayago** (Zamora), and **Deleitosa** (Cáceres), which as of now—1977—are no longer being made.

As for figured weaves of diverse texture, they are still being made with dignity and beauty in the Manchegan area of Albacete, in **Yeste, El Ballestero, Elche de la Sierra,** and **El Bonillo.** In this last town, the Rubio family, of long-standing textile tradition, dyes the wool using the traditional system, achieving the colors and tones of the old wools. In the Maestrazgo area, of rich textile tradition, there are active looms in

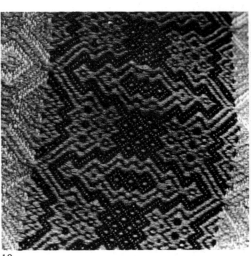

19

18

17   The dignified Galician coverlets are a fine example of the variety of decoration achieved with the "gorullo" technique

18   Detail of a saddlebag from Zamora

19   Figured weave coverlet. Morella, Castellón

23

Iglesuela del Cid (Teruel) and **Morella** (Castellón), which was renowned for its figured saddle-bags and blankets; the present production of the latter town has completely adulterated traditional coloring and method; they use wool mixed with acrylic and bright, unshaded colors, and work to satisfy the demands of a tourist market ill-informed regarding the true characteristics of Morella's artisan tradition.

Special weaves
There are several curious weaves we should like to summarize separately, as they are not among the textile forms we have found throughout the peninsula.

Vertical loom. All the types of weaving we have mentioned are done on horizontal looms; we should note that the broad cruppers for pack-saddles, which are still being made in Baeza to adorn beasts of burden, are made on a small vertical loom, with warp and woof of hemp and dyed wool of gay colors. (In the section on harness-making, we mention the work done by Barbara Aitken on this type of loom, presented to the First Congress of Folk Arts in Prague, in 1928.)

"Tongue" weave. This has been done only in Majorca and seems to have originated there with the Arabs, who brought the technique from Asia Minor, as there was already weaving on the island at the time of the Arab occupation. That this technique should be maintained by the women weavers of the island is remarkable, if we remember that Majorca, as a Mediterranean island, has always been an area of great French and Italian influence.
This is a plain, blue and white cloth, with warp and woof of the same fiber, and with no variation in the movement

20

of the shuttle. The warp is dyed in short, uneven blue stripes, dipping both ends of the skein; the woof is all blue, so that the finished fabric has up-and-down streaks of marbled blue, from which it gets its name. Presently, these cloths are still being made by hand in **Lloseta** and in **Pollensa**, in linen. There must have been abundant production on the island, as this cloth was used to cover beds and make curtains, cushions, and even mattresses. In **Sóller**, which had an important silk industry in the eighteenth century, these cloths were made in silk for more luxurious uses.
Another cloth worth mentioning, since after a splendorous past it barely survives, is a kind of heavy silk, made on a hand loom. The only place which still has silk looms is **El Paso**, island of La Palma, in the Canary Islands. The modest beauty of this cloth comes from the quality of the fiber, with which small handkerchiefs are made to be sold

20　Part of the production of Morella has degenerated in coloring and in the use of synthetic fibers

21　Saddle-bags and blankets are sold in the market in Morella

22

23

as souvenirs, or magnificent cloths destined for royal garments.

Feather rugs. This is a curious article which, in all of Spain, we have found only in the Viana del Bollo region, in **San Martín,** where Esperanza Rodríguez, skillful creator of woven and knit coverlets, inserts chicken feathers she has dyed herself into a plain weave, so that they stand out from the cloth. It seems that in a nearby village there is another weaver who also practices the technique. They call them rugs, perhaps because they cannot be made very large, and they must be kept flat. The technique has been attributed to some long-ago Spaniard's having returned from the New World after seeing the feathered cloths of Mexico; we are inclined to consider it a Celtic survival, as there are also feathered cloths in the northeastern part of Portugal, although the ones we saw used un-dyed feathers.

Cloth made from scraps
In many places in Castile, Galicia, and the Canary Islands, they used to make cloth using leftovers, for purely utilitarian purposes in the fields or in the homes: blankets for gathering grain, aprons for domestic chores, mats for the entrances to the houses, etc. They were woven on the same looms used for other, ornamental fabrics, but for these, strips of used linen or leftover wool were used. The designs were very interesting and might form squares, zig-zags, and use combinations of colors. They were and are given various names in each region: *"farrapeiras"* or *"mantarras"* in Galicia; *"retaleras"*, *"traperas"*, *"pingueras"*, and *"tiranas"* in Castile; and *"jarapas"* or *"harapas"* in Andalusia. Most of these names refer to the "remnants", "rags", or "scraps" of which the cloth was made, evoking its humble origin in recycling waste. This way of getting the most use out of materials is used on almost all

22   *Fabric from vertical loom, in colored wool, used for girths*

23   *Silk kerchief. Island of La Palma*

24   *Heavy coverlet. Galicia*

household looms, and in small factories which make only this cloth with horizontal stripes, without selecting colors, and using inferior quality or synthetic industrial textiles, and making the woof so thick it loses all proportion with the warp. The result is cloth of little consistency or durability. One can still find well made "*farrapeiras*" in Galicia, with the warp of flax, the strips for the woof slender, and the weave tight (in **Robra,** near Otero del Rey, in **Fornelos,** and in many other towns in which the "wool-weavers" take orders from their neighbors, making simple coverlets and curtains with the materials given them). Also in Cáceres, in **Ciudad Rodrigo,** and in **Deleitosa,** they produce well made blankets with scrap, as well as in Granada and Almería, in the villages of the Alpujarra region; in the province of Albacete, and on the island of La Gomera. But this represents the last step in the degeneration and impoverishment of the art of the loom. Another example of using otherwise unusable scraps is patchwork cloth, much used in the United States, and which in countries with a textile tradition must be considered evidence of poverty, in spite of the beautiful

27

26

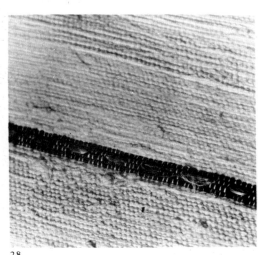

28

25   *Fabric with dyed feathers incorporated in the woof. Viana del Bollo, Orense*

26   *Fabric woven from strips of cloth—"farrapas". Galicia*

27, 28   *Two examples of the technique of making blankets by recycling materials*

results that can be got by combining different remnants, as in the small rugs made in Ibiza, in which the patches, folded to form a point, are sewn together forming pointed petals and, in a concentric design, create great, flattened flowers. Or the coverlets made with remnants, which are given a rounded shape and sewn with loose stitches, creating empty spaces.

Mechanical weaves of traditional design
We should like to make mention of an aspect which does not properly fall into the category of "artisan", a term deprived of its original meaning—which must be restored—or "made by hand", although this refers only to its material execution and does not suppose any underlying popular or "folk" spirit; this aspect is that of "traditional or folk designs", which industry launched at some moment, leaning surely on the weight of tradition and which has managed to replace the tradition that inspired it, or to create enough popularity so that it is considered traditional. We could speak here of the large kerchiefs which most likely had their origin in the textile factories of Catalonia. Now they are used throughout the peninsula to wrap things and make bundles of clothing which can be easily transported. The colors are shades of ochre and black, with lines that cross. Or the "homespun" handkerchiefs, similar in design, but in blue, sold at low prices in local markets; the ravens' duck sail cloth used in harness-making or as blankets and shelters for livestock, in shades of brown; the cinches with colored stripes; the small-print percales with black background which for years have been the fabrics used by village women for their skirts; and an endless variety of other designs which have come to be of general use in a region or to be inseparably associated with a given function.

29

29 *Large kerchief, used for carrying bundles, in a shop window. Barcelona*

30 *Embroidery on an antique shawl*

31 *Detail of open-work embroidery*

embroidery

30

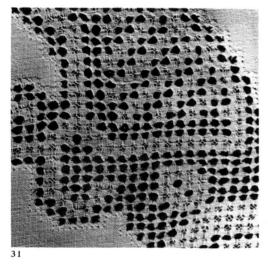

31

This is indeed an important chapter in the history of textile arts in Spain. Its importance is evident not only in the richness of the embroidery of the traditional folk dress of the various regions, used until the end of the nineteenth century, but in the profusion of needlework that adorned shirts, sheets, decorative pillows for beds, altar cloths, coverlets, and towels, which, while not an outward sign of the kind of dress, show a pronounced artistic and decorative taste.

There is also a rich tradition of embroidery made to be used by the nobility and the Church, which, as is natural, given that the educated classes are followers of fashion, has been subject to various influences. After a clearly oriental ornamentation—the flag named Las Navas de Tolosa—there followed French, Flemish, and Italian influences. The principal centers of embroidery for upper-class use were Seville, Toledo, extending to Guadalupe, León, Burgos, and Barcelona, which influenced the production of Valencia and Majorca. This elegant embroidery is done with silks; the technique is free, as the embroidery is done over a pre-fixed design, embellished with a great richness of shades and variety of techniques.

True folk embroidery, however, done essentially in the villages, uses only a few stitches, those usually found in other countries: plain embroidery, back stitch, cross stitch, and open work. This is because the embroiderers were conditioned to and helped by the homespun linen with thick warp and woof, which imposed the procedure of counting threads; that is, the design was achieved by counting the threads caught by the needle. Nor was there a great variety of colored threads, since these also were home-made or otherwise limited; silk was used little and cotton, less. The tradition of the designs, which are peculiar to Spain and show the combination of Moorish and Christian influence, has been preserved, as the young embroiderers followed the line of least resistance and found it easier to copy the designs from another piece by counting threads than to invent a new design. Trade with the New World had some influence, as in the importation in the eighteenth century of objects from the Philippines and China—especially the large shawls from Manila—but in general, popular Spanish embroidery remained faithful to its religious designs, such as symbols of the Passion; or oriental ones: geometric, two birds facing each other, fountains, and trees or plants, which have their origin in the Persian *tree of life*.

We shall try to classify techniques and designs by the areas in which they were, and are, made, but keeping in mind that in some areas there has been such commercialization that they no longer represent traditional regional designs, while in others, embroidery is sporadic and hardly done at all except as a pastime which follows the patterns it already knows.

The simple techniques of counted threads and openwork mentioned above can be explained as follows: Counted threads is a method used in plain embroidery, fill-in—which is plain embroidery that fills in a line left blank by an embroidered outline—and cross-stitch. Open work may be done by drawing out threads only from the woof or from the warp and grouping them to reinforce the cloth, which makes a thick openwork—which is also found in Sicily; or drawing out threads from both warp and woof, which results in pronounced squares which are filled in by another thread worked with the needle, creating lovely wheel or sun-like designs, like very open lace. This technique seems to come from Seville as a complicated derivation of Venetian lace, and later spread to the Canary Islands and America.

Toledan embroidery. Under this heading we include an important area of embroidery, which at present is very commercialized, called "Lagartera embroidery", after the town of that name. Today it provides work for village women in the provinces of Avila and Cáceres. They follow to some degree, with very adulterated designs and very standardized colors, the old tradition of geometric embroidery and open work. Both plain embroidery, in two colors and with symmetrical designs, which may be either geometric or stylized floral motifs (in which several colors are used) such as the acorn design, and open work, which is usually white on white, or natural or gray on white, have lost the delicacy, minute detail and richness of design that characterized them, since the production of table linen and decorative cloths is for use in the cities, where consumers are undemanding and unappreciative of traditional arts. The splendid old embroidery of the collars of village blouses, in black and common to the whole area, are being lost, as well as the polychromed embroidery in *"puntaditas"* ("little stitches") that were done in Oropesa, and the *"tejidillos"* ("little weaving") of Navalcán, a delicate embroidery done on the wrong side of the cloth which appeared lightly to blend together the elements of a brighter, more striking decoration.

Salamanca and Segovia. This wide area has used and uses the Persian designs of the tree of life, stylized in a thousand different ways, the lion (called "dog" here), and other animal forms, together with floral stylizations— carnation and pine—done in plain embroidery and cross-stitch. The old forms of distribution of the ornament are preserved, as these are not in such demand as Toledo embroidery, and the typical colors—honey, blue, red, and black—are still used, although somewhat brighter. The geometric patterns are very dense, and done in straight lines, following the form of the cloth, leaving wide unembroidered areas, or with designs in the corners. This austere yet rich embroidery was used on men's and women's shirts, tablecloths, offerings, and sheets; today it is used in tablelinen, tray doilies, and aprons.

32

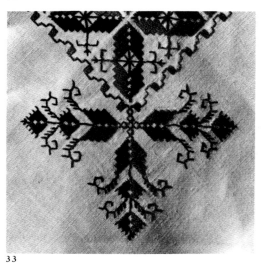

33

34

Zamora. In this region, the Carbajales embroidery, bright colors on a black background, is still done. It had been used to adorn the skirts of the women of Carbajales, and was done on black woven cloth or felt. The designs are large and separated, a result of having been done exclusively on wool. The embroidery being done today is used for drapes or hangings or round, floor-length tablecloths, and the colors are vivid. While traditional coloring was more limited and of muted tones, today, industrially dyed wools make brighter cloths, widely accepted but not traditional.

Majorca. In Artá and in Palma, they used to do a blue embroidery called "Majorcan stitch", creating stylizations of the leaves of the *parra,* a local vine, palm trees, and pines. This type of embroidery has been lost and the skilled hands of artisans now work on fine linens, producing the designs in fashion.

Andalusia. The characteristic embroidery of the province of Huelva, in Alosno and Puebla de Guzmán, is called *"cortadillo",* and is open embroidery on the cloth, which is turned under and bordered. For some years this type of openwork embroidery

36

37

35

32   Solid embroidery with geometric floral stylization

33   Typical Toledan embroidery showing fine combination of design and color

34   The embroiderers of Lagartera at work at the doors of their homes. Lagartera, Toledo

35   Woolen embroidery. Carvajales, Málaga

36, 37   Baroque embroidery, using traditional animal motifs

38

39

38   Young embroiderer at work on a set of openwork table linen in a workshop in Ingenio. Taller Ingenio, Great Canary Island

39   Table linen with openwork design

40   Woolen pockets and skirt with colored appliqués

41   Antique yellow woolen skirt from Zamora with appliqué designs

42   Ornate processional mantle of the Virgen de la Macarena, with aristocratic embroidery. Seville

was fashionable in table linen used in the cities, and was done in all the villages where there were embroiderers, so today it is hard to tell what its exact origin was.

The old embroidery on shirts, which in all of Castile is found in black or dark blue on white, alternating designs with openwork, is found here in red and green with such motifs as the Agnus Dei or the eagle in profile.

Canary Islands. In all the islands, embroidery has been greatly motivated by the northern European tourist trade, a good client of these handicrafts. Embroidered coverlets, table linen, tray doilies, and handkerchiefs are made for sale to tourists, following the traditional island style of openwork with *"randas"* or sun patterns in the open part, and Richelieu embroidery. The finest or most creditable embroidery is done in Orotava (Tenerife) and Ingenio (Grand Canary Island), and on the entire island of Palma. But in an

undeveloped area dependent on tourism as these islands are, it is to be expected that many villages take advantage of the possibility of selling "handicrafts", so that the art of embroidery has become a local "industry".

In **Galicia, Asturias,** and the **Basque Country,** embroidery has never been particularly significant; to be sure, there has been embroidery, but the designs have always been simple and of one or two colors, although really related to the popular ornamental tendencies seen in other techniques.

In **Catalonia, Valencia,** and **Murcia,** there is no distinctive folk tradition in embroidery; these areas have been much influenced by the tastes of the upper classes and therefore by changing fashion. Typical regional dress has been based more on the elegance of the fabrics than in their embellishment with embroidery in the folk tradition.

40

41

42

Other aspects of embroidery and adornments

There is a technique we have not yet described and which has been used for adorning plain cloth as well as in making fine embroidered linens: the appliqué. This consists of cutting out shapes of one texture or color and superimposing them on another. The most highly developed and distinctive examples of appliqué that we have seen are the traditional skirts of the Zamora region, in red on a yellow background, and the bedroom footstools in all of western Castile. Floral and animal motifs of Moorish—or Christian—origin were sewn on with tiny stitches and turned under if the consistency of the cloth permitted, and the edge bordered. We have found only one example of this technique's uninterrupted use, in the handbags still made in Valverde de la Vera (Cáceres), and another, though not traditional, application, in the hats of Montehermoso.

Other embroideries of the folk tradition, which require little technique but great care, are those done with thick braid, sequins and metallic threads, which have been used for years for small, precious, objects: reliquaries, frames for religious images, brides' handbags, which were a simple and ingenuous transposition of the ostentation of other social groups. Related to these, but with its own specific characteristics, is the adornment of bullfighters' dress, which includes embroidery and lace appliqué. Bullfighters' costumes have changed considerably since the last century, and the constants of color and ostentation have been accentuated. The making of this sort of costume requires specialized tailors, most of whom are found in Seville, Madrid, and Barcelona. The embroidery that adorns these costumes is in black or gold, contrasting or blending with the delicate or bold tones of the shiny cloth.

Embroidery in silk, with naturalist tendencies and a richness of shadings, are of upper-class origin, but find a popular projection in procession banners, the insignia of religious lay brotherhoods (*cofradías*), and costumes for religious statues. There are workshops specialized in these complex embroideries in **Murcia, Lorca, Málaga,** and **Seville**.

Fringes, tassels, and other trimmings deserve special mention. Most likely because of the Moorish influence (the "macramé" technique is Arabic), the profusion of fringes and their technique is more complex than in other countries. There isn't a coverlet or a towel that isn't trimmed with fringe and often it has tassels. Fringe was made either separately, or from the warp and woof of the fabric, braiding and interweaving the strands.

True macramé of thick cord and knots is widely used in making adornments for animals, as are tassels.

35

43

44

45

43　Silk girths and tassels for adorning horses. Seville

44　In Mula the coverlet and blanket industry requires a parallel industry of passementerie-work fringe. Mula, Murcia

45　Part of the embroidered jacket of a bullfighter's garb.

46　Frogs and sequins enrich the luxurious embroidery of bullfighters' suits

47　Simple folk embroidery. Toledo

48　A lace-maker of Camariñas, La Corunna, at work

lace

50

49 *Detail of the lace*

50 *Detail of the technique*

51 *The coarse bone-lace bobbins of Almagro, Ciudad Real, in the hands of the lace-maker*

52 *Traditional shop where patterns, models, bobbins, and cushions are sold. Barcelona*

With the graphic Italian expression *"punto in aria"* ("stitch in air") it's easy to describe what lace is: the creation of a decorative cloth without a previous net of supporting fabric. The technique, which has its origin in Italy, from where it spread to France—with a needle—and to the Low Countries —with bobbins—also reached Spain, where it was destined for use by refined members of society. Lace-making has been confined largely to the home and done exclusively by women, although until it was prohibited in the seventeenth century, lace was made in silver and gold, so there were large

centers of production and an organized market.

In spite of the changes which this artisan, household industry had to face when lace-making—in cotton thread, or blonde lace, with silk—became industrially mechanized, it has persisted with some strength in some parts of the peninsula: **La Corunna**, **Ciudad Real**, and **Barcelona** are still lace-producing centers.

The production of blonde and cotton lace has been limited in design, size, and materials used since ways of dress changed after the First World War. At the time of this writing, lace is used to adorn table linen, sheets, handkerchiefs, and feminine underclothes, and is bound to disappear soon, as there is no domestic demand and, except in a few places where the work of several lace-makers has been organized and is exported, as in **Almagro** (Ciudad Real), lace-making has been gradually disappearing. (In **Huércal-Overa** in Almería, **Monóvar** and **Novelda** in Alicante, **Acebo** in Cáceres, and even in Catalonia where there was a strong, established commercialization of hand-made lace, the number of persons dedicated to this work has decreased considerably and there is little possibility of maintaining tradition and technique in new generations.)

There are two techniques for making lace: the needle technique, in which a single thread moves from one point to another, its back-and-forth movement creating the design, and the bobbin technique, in which several threads are interwoven. The former had its start in Venice and spread from there to France.

In Spain, needle-made lace is used for the ornamental designs made in the Canary Islands. A very famous lace is that of **Vilaflor**, in Tenerife, which is similar to Venetian lace. In both Lanzarote and Tenerife, many women

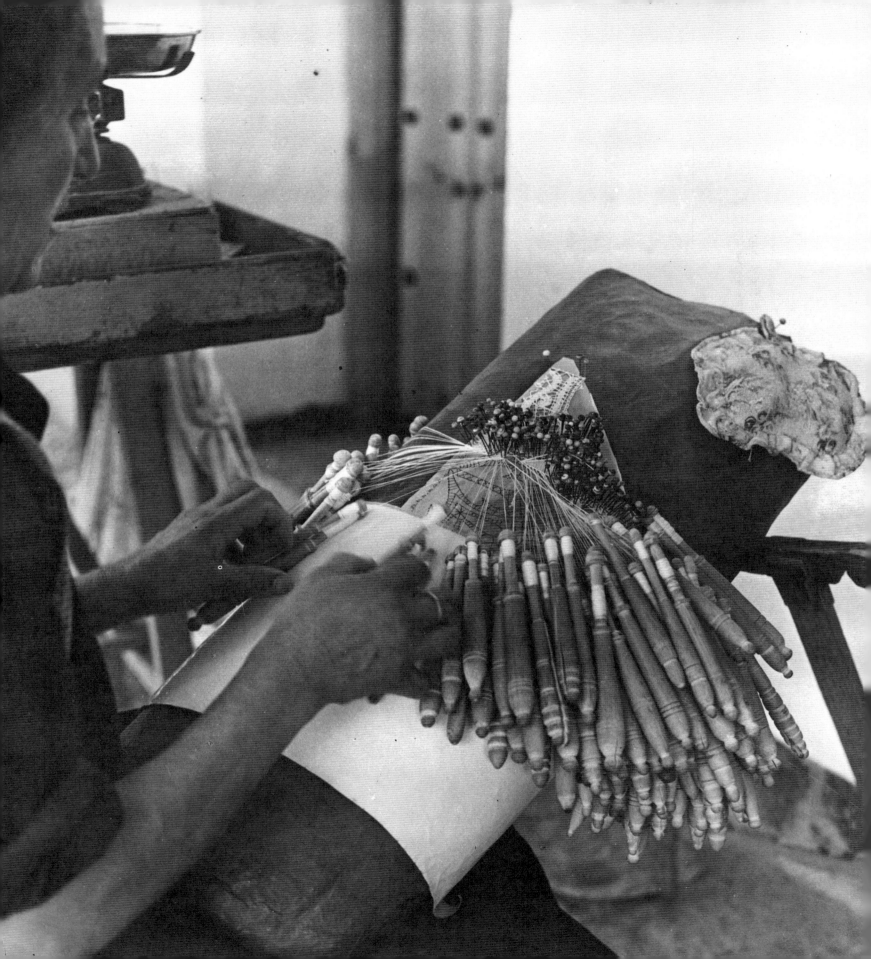

work at making the famous needle-worked lace "roses" or "rosettes", in white or unbleached thread. These are then joined together to make coverlets or inlaid in fabric. In Ariana, this weave is done over a tin pattern which serves as a guide for the design. It has holes for the pins which, stuck into the pillow over which the lace is made, serve to hold the threads in place as the beautiful design is created. The relative increase in tourism from northern islands has given a boost to this traditional industry.

Bone-lace requires three elements each of which almost has a personality of its own: first, the pillow, usually covered with red or green *"lustrina"*, a cloth similar to alpaca. In Spain, this pillow is oval, while in other countries that produce lace it is round, with a little box to hold the lace. The bobbins which hold the thread may be of olive, boxwood, or almond wood. Some, used for over a generation, are shiny from time and use. The pieces of cardboard, on which the design is pricked out, are red. Some of them, of complicated and laborious design, have been objects of "artisan espionage" by families who make lace, for having an exclusive design improved sales possibilities. During the decade from 1920 to 1930,

bone-lace making was commonly taught in the schools, since in addition to being a virtuous activity—it requires much patience, cleanliness, and orderliness—it was considered of pegadogical value.

The lace made in schools was simple, and the cardboard patterns were bought, along with the pillow and bobbins, in stores dealing in lace; these necessary items were accompanied by a bit of lace already begun which served to show better the results of the cardboard being bought.

In Galicia, lace-making is centered in **Camariñas** and surrounding fishing villages in La Corunna. The lace-makers, working with their patterns, make beautiful, thick, tightly-knitted lace, which they themselves take to the capital to sell, or sell in the villages. It is not a profitable business, and emigration continues, but in Camariñas or in Muxía there are still grandmothers who teach their granddaughters the secrets of bone-lace and its designs: suns, stars, flowers, crosses, animals, and geometric figures.

In the province of Ciudad Real there are several villages with a long-standing tradition of lace-making: **Granátula, Moral de Calatrava, Almagro.** In Almagro, one of the towns which has

produced the most and best lace, the work of more than five hundred women from Almagro and other towns is centralized. In this area, with sturdy bobbins of olive wood, spool-thread lace and silk *mantillas* are made.

In the coastal area of Catalonia, from Gerona to Tarragona, there is a long tradition of making bone-lace. Barcelona, rich and prosperous city, put together a flourishing business, which gave impulse to lace-making, especially in black silk—blonde lace— for two centuries, and even exported blonde lace. So established and popular was the figure of the lace-maker of Catalonia, that she appeared in many plays, narratives, and musical works in the late nineteenth century.

We find lace-makers in the streets of **Palamós,** in **Arenys de Mar** and **Arenys de Munt, Olot, Arbós del Penedés,** sitting outdoors, with their bobbins dancing rhythmically. But here, too, the tradition is dying out. A symptom of this consciousness and the attempt to keep all this knowledge alive are the efforts of the Raventós sisters to star a school for lace-makers, which has been established in a school in Barcelona, and a book they have published, which studies the history of this industry and the peculiarities of seventy different styles.

basket making and work with palm

53

54

53   Robust cane and wicker baskets for rural use. Hierro, Tenerife

54   Men spinning esparto for making the cord. Cieza, Murcia

55   Strips of braided raw esparto are joined to make the great panniers used in the country. La Solana, Ciudad Real

With the same vision that guided us in this tour through the world of popular forms and techniques, we include the area of basket-making and other arts done with plant fibers and textile methods, such as rural hats and caps, rope-soled sandals, called *"alpargatas"*, floor mats, and the beautiful palm structures used to celebrate Palm Sunday.

Basket-Making

Something so humble and ordinary as basket-weaving still is has very seldom been taken as an object of study by students of folk arts (although it has been studied by ethnologists), since the products of Spanish basket-making have been traditionally utilitarian, and only on a very few occasions have there been objects made for ornamental purposes. Unlike the delicate Sardinian baskets of stylized decoration, or the extraordinary works of art of the American Hopi Indians, and so many peoples who have developed an art of plant weaving, our basket-making merely forms a part of rural occupations, done without esthetic considerations, but which in our view appears valuable, as much for the vigorous forms the products are given as for the techniques used.

We refer here to basketry made by rural artisans, whose market includes the farmers or fishermen of limited areas, and who sell their wares at local fairs and markets; or to articles made by the farmers themselves for their most immediate needs. Thus, we can group items geographically according to materials used, since each area adopts the most abundant raw materials for use.

Andalusia and Extremadura. In extensive Andalusia we see many wicker baskets made with olive and

unpeeled willow, which are used for gathering harvests from the field or for transporting things: *espuertas,* which are frails with two handles; baskets for gathering vintage; large frails or baskets called *capazos,* and an infinite variety of receptacles for keeping cereal grain.

They are strong, dignified, durable pieces, well suited to their functions. With fibers that are more flexible and therefore easier to work with, and with softer shapes, we find other kinds of baskets for household use, such as the delicate baskets of **Níjar** and **Alhabia** in the province of Almería, made with very fine esparto, or grass hemp, and in which color is used as interwoven border design and handles and edges are of great delicacy considering the humble quality of the fiber; they are used for keeping eggs, for shopping, for keeping bread and for other household needs. The esparto, which grows wild in the dry areas of the

56

57

58

56   "Aguaderas", *esparto baskets used to transport large jugs of water or other products. Berja, Almería*

57   "Cofines", *made of esparto, used here to dry dates. Elche, Alicante*

58   *A recent craft is the making of rugs from boiled esparto. Ubeda, Jaén*

59   *Bundles of osier are sold in markets and rural fairs*

61

60   *Baskets of palmetto have a wide market. Gata de Gorgos, Alicante*

61   *Esparto and wicker panniers are used in harvesting grapes. Tomelloso, Ciudad Real*

peninsula, is even cultivated sometimes, since it is also used in the paper industry as raw material. Its stem is hard, resistant, and slender, and can be worked with certain ease, braiding it and then braiding the braids, called plaits, together. Thus, articles are formed ranging from the huge hampers used to carry merchandise by horseback—like soft canoes that adapt themselves to the back of the animal and form two nests on either side of the body—to the curious flat baskets used to press ground olives to extract the oil, called *"cofines"*, which are made on a sort of rudimentary loom,

in circular weave, with a large opening for putting the olives in and a small opening in the center of the back for the press. Although the stitch used in making the *"cofín"* is called the Artana stitch (Artana is a town in the province of Castellón), which seems to clearly indicate its origin, at present the main production of this basket is in the villages of the province of Jaén, especially in the town of **Ubeda,** where there has also appeared a subindustry of souvenirs made with the same material. With the technique of working with "plaits", which are flat braids of any length, rolled up,

62

63

64

innumerable objects are made, such as heads of mules, whose only relation to basketry is in the material used.
Split reeds produce a more fragile and angular basketry, as the dried reed is brittle and is combined with unpeeled willow. As it is a poor material and easily worked, it is the most used by the nomad gypsy basket-makers. The gypsy population has become more sedentary, but it preserves in part—since many of its members work as day-laborers at seasonal work—its old activities and professions, among them that of the basket-makers. Gypsy basket work in fine wicker and rushes

or reeds is graceful and colorful, almost always destined for household use and of small sizes: baskets for taking animals to market, for vegetables and eggs, with round lid joined to the handles, little baskets with arabesques as finishing, and other articles which are called "embroidered baskets". In Extremadura we should note the work in chestnut bark, with which square baskets are made, with warp and woof usually of the same thickness. It is curious to note the artisan's need for adornment; after the complete process of making the basket, the sides are decorated by wood-burning.

65

66

In **Salamanca**, there is a village with a large basket production to meet household needs, and production of wicker chairs. This is the town of **Villoruela**, which sends clothes baskets, ironing trays, and chairs of boiled wicker to all of Spain.

The Mediterranean Coast and the Balearic Islands. The most typical production of this Mediterranean area is the work with palmetto, a plant of the palm family, which grows fan-shaped with leaves two meters high in non-cultivated areas in the provinces of Levante and Majorca.

These leaves, once whitened with hot sulfur, are torn into strips and are an excellent material, durable and pliable, with which many different kinds of articles are made: from dainty little baskets, with strips of palmetto dyed bright colors, to durable baskets, used for packing oranges. The area of most concentrated production is that of **Capdepera, Pollensa,** and **Alcudia** (Majorca), which must import the palmetto leaves from Alicante and Almería, as this area has achieved a broad commercialization of mats, baskets, and a kind of basket which is hung from the shoulder. These are

used not only in the islands but in cities on the peninsula.

In **Gata de Gorgos** (Alicante) there was a local production specialized in palmetto plaits and one can still see women who, besides their housework, work at braiding this fiber, which they then sell to small family workshops where they are made into large frails, baskets for shopping, etc. In recent years and facilitated by already existing basket factories, there has developed a healthy industry of plant fiber furniture, but not with local raw materials, nor traditional designs; both raw materials and design are imported, and the final products are exported to American and European markets which order well-made merchandise from these skilled artisans. These important and dependable orders have phased out the manufacture of various articles of boiled wicker (put in boiling water, it turns a dark golden color), comfortably shaped, and with attractive interwoven designs, which once filled the peaceful patios of coastal villages. There are still some artisans who make them and sell them in basket shops and other shops in the cities: chairs for children, candle-tables and other tables, and high-backed chairs with wide arms. In this area, especially on the coast and inland in the Levantine area (from **Murcia** to the mountains of **Castellón**), esparto fills the same agricultural needs we have seen in Andalusia, but, as there are crops peculiar to the area, we find extraordinary examples of material and form suited to function: very large, lightweight baskets, with much open work and a very large handle, which have been used in the flat fields of Murcia for picking white mulberry leaves and other products of great volume and little weight. They were hung from the shoulder and the leaves could be stored and aired without moving them to another container. We must also mention the durable *alpargatas,* shoes or sandals made of esparto, used in all sorts of farm work, but especially in growing rice, since the fiber is compact and water-resistant. In **Elche** (Alicante), they prepare the palm branches which later are made into the beautiful structures used on Palm Sunday. Throughout the year, the large palm grove is cared for and the leaves covered or "hooded" with the leaves of past years so that the sun and light will not turn them green. The entire crop is destined for this purpose and, aside from the filigree work done in Elche itself, it is sent in the form of large palm branches, whitened with

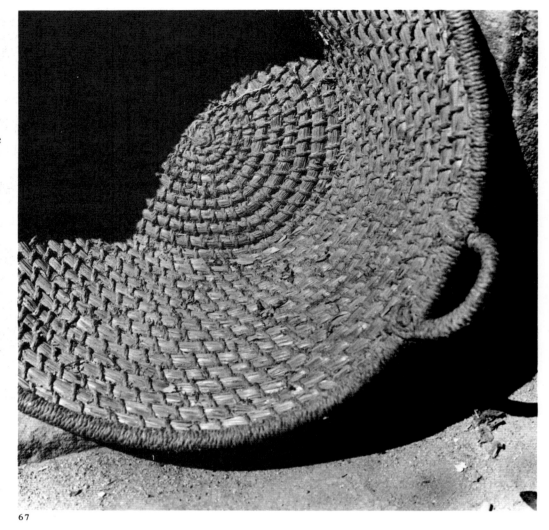

67

sulfur and dampened so that the fiber can be worked, to storage in Barcelona, Gerona, and Tarragona, which is where the most exquisite articles are made and sold.

The Castilian Plateau and León. In the central part of the peninsula, the technique of weaving unthrashed wheat or rye straw in a spiral has been preserved until recently. This technique, characteristic of northern European countries, is now used only in remote villages, such as **Lucillo,** in the province of León. It is most interesting because it has perpetuated a very primitive form

of the art of basket-weaving over thousands of years, and we find very old, or little-changed, shapes, such as the *"escriño",* an immense jug-shaped hamper for keeping ceral grains, and a sort of very wide-mouthed bowl. The dry stems of straw are twisted and coiled and then sewn with thin thongs of birch or blackberry bark, beginning at the bottom and following the coil. The result is extraordinary for the archaic harmony of the forms, the warm, golden color of the material, and the beauty of the technique. The coil method of basket-making is also found in the Pyrenees area—but no

68

longer used—and is still being practiced in the Canary Islands.

In Cuenca and Guadalajara, osier, the willow used in wicker, is cultivated extensively. The red stems, separated according to length, are sent to the rest of the country, where local basket-makers, small furniture industries, or other small factories of more standardized production (grocery baskets, *cuévanos*—large baskets wider at the top than at the bottom—for transporting goods, baskets for bottles, etc.) work with them, cutting them in sections, peeling them to expose the white pulp or to dye them by boiling.

Last, they are made into, perhaps, durable panniers, vintage baskets, compost baskets, or into the "cherry" baskets we see in the vineyards of Toro or in the fields along the banks of the Ebro.

The Basque Country, Cantabrian area, and Galicia. In this large, damp and rainy area, chestnut and hazel-nut wood, in strips of varying thicknesses, are used in basket-making. The consistency of the material determines the method of working with it, and due to consistency and technique, the shapes are open and solid. The bottoms

67   *Fragment of an old straw basket*

68   *Braiding raw esparto. Ayna, Albacete*

55

69

69   Basket of coarse, unpeeled wicker.
Muros, La Corunna

70   Galician markets boast a rich display
of basketry. Noya, La Corunna

71   Lovely, durable chestnut "cuévanos".
Ribadavia, Orense

70

of the baskets are wide and, as warp and woof are very stiff, the sides are straight, and so must be finished with a hoop at the top which holds in the strips of chestnut and also serves as handle. Among the baskets made with this technique is the *"cuévano"*, which used to be used for carrying babies on the back, fastening the *cuévano* with two straps crossed over the chest. Today, while still presenting the same medieval image, it is used for gathering and transporting grass. Smaller baskets are the Basque-Navarran *"espuerta"*, much used in harvesting and transporting farm products, and the flat baskets for various uses. The same materials and technique are used in making grain storage bins in Asturias. In Galicia, where parishes and villages still live the rural culture of self-sufficiency, there is an enormous profusion of baskets, including *cuévanos* and *espuertas,* made with the most varied materials and techniques. A weekly fair or market in a Galician town is a true festival of baskets: an abundance of large square baskets of chestnut, whitened or variegated with alternating shades, with a high handle which can be removed, as it also is made of chestnut and is tightly fit into the woof of the basket; wide baskets of unpeeled wicker, made by the *"costillar"* method which consists of covering an oval formation of staves with sticks arched like the keel of a boat, which forms a sort of bread basket or tray; baskets of rye straw sewn with blackberry, following the coil method and with a reinforced base; baskets for vegetables, rectangular, with high sides, made of chestnut strips; round trays for fish and shellfish, of peeled or unpeeled wicker or a combination of the two; and an infinite variety of baskets for household use.

We also find, but only in livestock fairs,

72

73

74

72   "Estrobos", *a peculiar addition to the yoke. Galicia*

73, 74   *Front and back of rain cape used in Galicia and northern Portugal*

75   *Baskets made with the circular technique. Andraitx, Majorca*

the *"estrobo"*, loop formed by a twisted green branch with which the oxen's yoke is fastened to the pole of the cart. Two curious techniques with quite different applications are also found in Galicia. In the province of Orense, one often sees cows grazing, covered with a cape of reeds or rye straw, used to protect the newly calved cow from the rain. These garments, called *"corozas"*, are also used by shepherds and consist of a braided vest over which layers of fringe are knotted. Rushes and rye straw repel the water which runs down into the fringe. (These capes are also used in the region of Minho, in Portugal, of similar culture.) Other curiosities are the pitchers and little cups for wine, covered inside with pitch. Today they are also sealed with industrial varnishes. This survival of such archaic vessels is most strange, because Galicia has prestigious potteries whose wares are widely sold at local markets and livestock fairs.

The Pyrenees area and Catalonia. In the mountainous area of Huesca, Lérida, and Gerona, there is a production similar to that in the Basque Country and Navarre, in strips of chestnut or birch, with the *costillar* technique and in which the keel or central axis is extended to form a handle on either side of the basket. These baskets are called *"paneres"* or *"banastes"*. There are interesting and varied baskets for taking products to market, made with osier and reeds, which are common in all farming areas: a single handle in the middle appears from within the framework and takes shape just at the edge of the basket, which has a truncated cone shape and is lightweight and easy to handle. Also in unpeeled wicker, there are very large baskets for transporting small animals; they are very spacious with a wide base, straight sides, and a lid with a lot of open work, so as to be able to see animals inside; the handle is

77

78

76 *Interior of a workshop where wicker furniture is made. Gata de Gorgos, Alicante*

77 *A "cuévano",* made of chestnut and *carried on the back. Vega de Pas, Santander*

78 *Great baskets for holding fish on a fishermen's wharf. Catalonia*

wide and the basket is carried over the arm. The "snail baskets", for keeping snails alive at home, have an interesting shape: wide-bellied with narrow neck, and a lid secured by a stick inserted through two rings on either side of the top. It has only one small handle for hanging.

All along the coast there are master craftsmen who make products used by fishermen: voluminous fish baskets of woven rushes, nearly a meter long, with a conical mouth which acts as a funnel; a lid of net allows the contents to be emptied. Others are lantern-shaped and of various sizes. These basket-makers also make panniers for fish and baskets for drying the long, thick cord to which several hooks are attached. This basket has a border of cattail—a flexible, cushioned material—where the several fish-hooks are stuck as in a pincushion.

There are also other baskets for household use and for use in fishing.

Canary Islands. In these islands we find straw baskets using the coil technique already described with reference to the *"escriños"* of Castile and León. Here, the most typical articles of this anachronistic basketry are the *"balayos",* large baskets with a very wide mouth, used to winnow cereals. Curiously, the word comes from the Portuguese *balaio,* which means broom, and which in turn comes from the Celtic *balazm.* The word *"balay"* is a generic name for basket in South America.

With the same technique using coiled straw and fine strips of bark, we find a sieve being used in La Laguna, called *"garnero",* with the bottom made of jonquil sewn together. (Sieves of this sort are also found in Sardinia and in Morocco.)

Also using wheat straw, we find lovely little boxes used by women. The form and technique of these boxes has fallen into disuse in the peninsula. The

61

79   *Making of a basket for holding fish.*
Catalonia

80   *Baskest for drying fishing lines. Costa*
Brava

81   *Hat seen in fields of Lanzarote*

80

technique consists of using the entire stem, without flattening or sectioning it, forming rigid little strips which are woven around two stays which serve as a framework. The result is a flat piece which can be combined with others in various ways. Then, the box is trimmed with straw, either braided or made into decorative rose shapes. Palm leaves are also used here, not for palms for Palm Sunday, but for mats, hats, and brooms.

Traditional rural hats

In some regions of Spain, the oldest inhabitatants still use the the delightful traditional hats in the villages and in the fields. Usually, it is the women who wear them, although in some places, such as the Sierra de Guadalupe area, in **Aldeanueva de San Bartolomé** (Toledo), both men and women use them. They are simple hats, of braided and sewn-together rye straw, oval-shaped and decorated in the front with a cockade of braided straw. A kerchief can be worn under the hat, or the brim turned up and kerchief worn over the hat. The same type of hat is also found elsewhere in the province of Toledo, as in Robledo del Mazo.

Other hats still in use include that of the Noya area in La Corunna. It is worn by women and has a wide brim, and a low crown with a black ribbon around it. These hats are made of whitened rye straw in the **Sierra de Outes** (La Corunna).

In the Canary Islands, they use hats of whitened palm stiffened with gum. There are slight differences in the shape from one island to another, but in general the hats have a wide, slightly drooping brim and high crown; they also can be worn with a kerchief underneath for better protection while doing farm work. A curious sight are the leathery-faced sailors of Lanzarote, sporting small delicate hats of palm leaves.

81

The triangle formed by Salamanca, Avila, and Segovia is another area of rye straw hats, similarly made and bearing the same sort of adornment: flowers, crosses, and rosettes of open straw and incorporating bits of cloth and straw cord. Generally, there is a wide visor reaching the sides, leaving the back free for the hair gathered in a knot. The cap is worn very straight. In **Cipérez** (Salamanca), the hat has a brim all the way around, with a little mirror in the middle and dangling adornments.

These hats are used only in some traditional dances or by elderly women.

However, there is a considerable production of hats sold as decorative objects or souvenirs. Consequently, the traditional forms were quickly abandoned; now colored paper and a motley assortment of superfluous adornments are used and the hats are carelessly made.

Another very beautiful sort of hat is that used in Cáceres, made in the Montehermoso Cooperative. It has a very high crown, and is adorned with cloth cut-outs and plaited straw. The coloring of the adornments varies with the age of the woman wearing the hat.

These hats are worn only by elderly women, who wear them daily. Thus, the brightly colored, decorated hats are made only for sale as souvenirs, so that traditional forms have been spoiled. Throughout the peninsula, one could see men and women working in the flat fields in summer, wearing broad-brimmed hats to protect them from the sun. The hats used by men and women were very similar, and were the same in La Mancha as in Andalusia: they came from Alicante and Murcia, were made of rough palmetto, and were wold by the hundreds in all the local markets. In only a few years, these

82   *Small box made of wheat straw with various kinds of braiding. Canary Islands*

83   *Hat of Avila*

84   *Hat of Montehermoso, Cáceres*

85   *Hats made in the Levantine region, with charming painted decoration. Alarcón, Cuenca*

82

64

83

84

hats have disappeared, replaced by hats imported from Brazil, China, and Colombia, and given form—on the old hatters' blocks used for the native hats—in the same places where the palmetto used to be harvested and worked.

A curious hat, if it can be called a hat, is the Catalonian *"gorra de cop"*, a cushioned hat of straw worn by young children to protect the head and ears from blows. It is spherical in shape and has as trimming a little open-work dome and ribbons, pink for girls and blue for boys.

Rope-soled shoes

This type of footwear, called *alpargatas*, and related to basketry, is common to the entire Mediterranean area. (Ohter types of footwear, such as wooden shoes and clogs, are related to leather and wood crafts and will be dealt with in another section.) All of these have a similar form: a sole of plant fiber, with a tip partially or completely covering the toes, a strap which shapes itself to the heel, and ribbons or cords tied over the instep. The ones used in Ibiza, called *"espardenyes"*, are especially interesting. They are made with very fine agave threads glued together to form a high, slightly curved toe; the heel is of the same material and delicate strands join heel and toe. Rather than peasant footwear, they seem the elegant shoes of a courtier. Quite the opposite of the delicate Ibizan *"espardenyes"* are the rough, durable *"esparteñas"* of Murcia. The name refers to the grass hemp, or esparto, of which they are entirely made. This shoe is found in Alicante, Valencia, and Castellón, as far as the mouth of the Ebro River, with curious names and slight variations. Thus, *"l'espardenya de careta"* of Valencia, used in rice paddies and orange groves, has a short toe covering only the toes.

85

The whole shoe is made of esparto and the pair is joined together by a slender cord which must be cut; this way pairs are not separated and they can be hung in storage. They are used only by men. Last, the most common sort of *alpargata,* used also in southern France: those with hemp soles and cloth uppers, which differ from one region to another in the placement of the cotton laces which tie them to feet and legs. As it is a cool and comfortable sort of shoe, it has come to be mass-produced, with changes in material and design, and is now common, standardized footwear sold in shoe stores.

Mats and rugs
In all areas where plaited basket-ware of flat fibers (palm, palmetto) is made, they make mats for household use. Some are plain, simply sewing the plait and applying another plait to the edge (**Artá, Capdepera**, in Majorca) and others

86

86   *The* alpargatas *of Ibiza*

87   *Making the hemp soles for* alpargatas. *Murcia*

88   *Shop selling rope-soled sandals in a small town. Cervera, Lérida*

66

87

are colored, dyeing the strips of palm or palmetto with analine, an artificial alkaloid (**Gata de Gorgos**, in Alicante), or simply using the different coloration of the leaves (**Lanzarote, La Graciosa**, in the Canary Islands). Esparto mats, using the technique of joining plaits together, are used to cover the poles which form the sides of animal-drawn carts, or to cover the stone floors of the spacious entrances of the houses.

Of a different sort are the worked rugs made of fine or boiled esparto, with open work. Those made in **Ubeda** (Jaen), **Guadix** (Granada), and **Cieza** (Murcia) are famous.

Palms and "palmones" for Palm Sunday

Traditionally, on Palm Sunday, children carry palm confections, called *palmas* and *palmones,* to religious services to be blessed, and the parents take laurel and olive branches. Later, all are hung on the balconies of the homes until the next year to prevent—according to tradition—certain misfortunes.

This custom originated with the commemoration of Jesus' arrival in Jerusalem, which the Roman Catholic Church adopted in the twentieth century, adding the blessing of the branches. Thus, the procession of the faithful to the doors of the temple, bearing branches of laurel, olive, boxwood and palm, and singing hymns, appeared as an act of liturgical ceremony.

In Catalonia and in the larger towns of Valencia, the custom of the worked palm branches appeared in the middle of the nineteenth century—it is said that the finely wrought article was first used in 1860 in a town near Barcelona, in the fertile area of Llobregat, and from there it spread to Barcelona, where the powerful basket-makers' guild sold and stimulated demand for this creation: a

89

90

89   Rugs of boiled and dyed esparto. This is not a traditional design

90   Traditional rural mats made with wide plaits of raw esparto. Ubeda, Jaén

91   In many Levantine and Majorcan towns, women work at braiding palmetto. Gata de Gorgos, Alicante

92   Women making the classic hats used in the villages near Puente del Arzobispo. Robledo del Mazo, Toledo

93   Coarse wicker basket for rural labors. Galicia

95

96

special way of working with and adorning these large palm branches with a filigree of construction and ornamentation that makes them true works of art.

The palm branches are sent, unworked, from Elche, where they are stored from early February; they must be kept damp so they can be worked. The work cannot be done until a few days before Holy Week because once plaited they quickly lose their elegance and they take up too much room to be able to keep them in a damp enough place. The feverish working against the clock begins some twenty days before Palm Sunday—which, furthermore, falls on different dates—and in some places, only a week before, if there is not a large market, or if several people can work at once. We should emphasize the highly seasonal nature of this work: at best, one month a year. And yet, it requires considerable storage facilities and enclosed areas to whiten the

finished palms with sulfur smoke. They are sold on the Friday and Saturday before Palm Sunday, and the lovely articles of finely wrought leaves appear in all their beauty only on the morning of Palm Sunday. All these elements make us appreciate all the more the survival of this work.

The center of production and the greatest market are in the city of Barcelona, although Elche, Valencia, and Lérida are also important centers. Some small family basket factories in Barcelona send palms to other large cities but the best, most ornate and refined ones are kept for the Feria de Palmones, which is installed each year on an avenue of the city. Among the most carefully made ones, it is hard to find two alike since, to the basic structure consisting of the branch itself and its leaves, braided without breaking them off from the branch, an infinite variety of adornments is added: stars, lilies, twisted cord, and spools. These

94   Detail of a palm with braiding and cut-out. Barcelona

95   The white strips of palm must be worked before they dry out

96   Ceremonial palm which will be used in the cathedral in Barcelona

are made separately and sewn to the main body. It is interesting to note that so sturdy is the work that palms can be up to a meter and a half high and of considerable diameter and the main elements of weave and structure come from the central branch.

The making of miniature palms is quite curious. They are most delicate and, in spite of their size, show the work and ornamental style of each artisan family, as in the case of the Fernández family.

The large branches, *palmones,* which are carried by children, compete in height and grace and are usually sold "as is", but there are innovations: the "combed palms" with shredded leaves, or the "braided palms" in which the leaves of the branch are braided.

Cages

Partridges abound in Spain and hunting them is a popular sport. Frequently, hunters keep young or full-grown partridges in cages in their homes to use as decoys. The cages are most often made of unpeeled wicker or curved branches from shrubs, and are round with straight sides and a cone-shaped top. The floor is made of woven sisal, agave cord, or wicker. These cages are found only locally, as those sold everywhere have the same shape, but are made of heavy wire.

In the **Canary Islands,** they make some beautiful cages of common reed-grass which adopt the forms of their typical architecture. Some of these cages, large enough to keep 15 or 20 birds, are crowned with two or three bell towers, in imitation of the colonial churches. The reed is worked whole, joining the bars which pass through the slits or holes made in the hollow stems. The result is very harmonious.

There are other types of cages as well, especially the peculiar ones used for raising canaries. They are made with fine strips of wood and delicate bars.

Brooms and mattress beaters

The wide gamut of traditional brooms, suitable for various needs, are being substituted by industrially made brooms and brushes, made of synthetics and having the same form. But one can still find some worthy varieties of this diligent article of witchery connotations.

In **Puente del Arzobispo** (Toledo), they make short brooms, archaic instruments made entirely of rye straw, attached at one end by a straw rope, without a handle. They are sold in pairs, attached together and, without the usual broomstick, they seem more like strange decorative objects.

In **Minorca,** they use small brooms or brushes for white-washing the houses. They are made of soft palmetto and are attached to a short handle with dyed strips.

The brooms used in the cities, as well as the fans for fanning the fire and balls of esparto used for scrubbing are made mostly in small workshops on the coast of Alicante, Málaga, and Murcia, and in Majorca. The modest workshops where they make these utensils, which, in spite of their simplicity, require several preparatory operations—combing the hanks of palmetto or *algarabía* (a wild plant), sorting them by length, tying them together, etc.—recall the scenes of nineteenth century industry described by Dickens: in a dark and dusty place, the young laborers work with rudimentary equipment.

There are also brooms of various shapes made of tamarisk and broom, which are used for sweeping paved and cobblestone streets. Mattress beaters seem, to the unaccustomed eye, like peculiar sorts of basketry. They are usually made of peeled or unpeeled wicker, but the artisans like to give them curious ornamental shapes, which don't affect their function, but make for a great variety.

97

97   *Perfect architecture of miniature palm*

98   *Braided palms forming rosettes in the fair at Palma*

99

100

99   *Mattress beaters in their curious forms*

100   *Brooms made of wheat straw. Puente del Arzobispo, Toledo*

pottery and ceramics

In Spain there are extensive and documented recent studies on the various forms of pottery still existing. Corredor-Matheos and Natacha Seseña have collaborated with enthusiasm and precision so that the Spanish public with an interest in the subject might have an up-to-date, sensitive, and exhaustive knowledge of the surviving forms of the *"barros y lozas de España"* ("earthenware and fine ceramics of Spain"—title of a work published by Seseña).

The variety of forms still found today, forming groups of pieces peculiar to a given area, the variety of techniques in use of the potter's wheel, and the wealth of decorative designs, make this folk art the most widespread, lively, and interesting of all.

We shall not attempt a very extensive treatment, but shall try to point out the most distinctive local forms, describing the differences in technique and form, noting the cultural memories that endure in many of them, and the different types of decoration, although only superficially.

GALICIA

Here we shall mention four pottery centers. There are four others in operation, but their production is not of great interest, and we prefer to concentrate on a few of interest.

In **Bonxe**, a small village near Otero del Rey (Lugo), there is only one artisan left. The pieces are very beautiful, full-shaped, and with delicate whitish designs on the edge of the glaze, which gives them a certain courtly air: jugs of various sizes, *botijos* (the peculiar Spanish water jugs, with a wide spout for pouring water in, a narrow spout for drinking, and a round handle for carrying), bowls for wine, wide-bellied pots and kettles with handles.

The pottery of **Mondoñedo** (Lugo) is simple. There, also, there remains but one potter, and he is hoping to quit

his craft. His is a more utilitarian and diversified production: cooking pots of various sizes, pitchers, cheese-drainers, little wine cups, baking pans, watering troughs for chickens, planters. The larger pieces are decorated with two parallel lines, which heightens the medieval appearance of the utensils. The potter sells his wares in local fairs.

In the province of Orense, there is a pottery still busy enough to last some years, in **Niñodaguia**, along the national highway. Here wide water jugs, wavy-mouthed jugs, butter pots, etc., are made, with a yellowish glaze which does not cover them entirely. The large water jugs are very round and simple, and all the pieces give an impression of fragility because with the clay used, the sides can be made very thin.

The utensils made in **Buño** (La Corunna) are the ones most used in Galicia. They are sold in all the traveling markets and in crockery shops in the cities; large pots with blunt handles, deep, straight-sided pans, *"cuncas"* and *"cunquelos"*, which are different kinds of bowls, "penny"-banks, and *"viradeiras"*, used to turn the delicious potato omelets made in

103

102

104

101   Ordinary cooking pot in the potter's hands. Mondoñedo, Lugo

102   Interior of a local crockery shop. Buño, La Corunna

103   Lovely jug from Niñodaguia, Orense

104   Ornamentation typical of Buño, La Corunna

105

106

105   *Burnished black earthenware* botijo.
Llamas de Mouro, Asturias

106   *Dignified incised decoration on a piece
from Llamas de Mouro, Asturias*

107   *The elderly mother of the last potter
still working in Bonxe, Lugo, with a* botijo
made by her son

the region. The glaze is rough, the decoration yellowish on a dark brown background, or dark brown on yellow, and consists of concentric circles or simple stylizations of plant motifs. There are also several non-traditional pieces.

ASTURIAS

This region had a significant history of pottery; at present, there are only two potteries; One is in **Faro,** and has modernized the wheel it had used and has stopped making the smoked pottery it once produced. The other is in **Llamas de Mouro.** Production there is limited as there is only one potter and he must divide his time between the pottery and his work in the fields, but he still makes magnificent pieces of smoked clay: beautifully turned *botijos* which, when almost dry, but before being put in the kiln, are "polished" by rubbing, which gives a shine to the surface. Once baked, they have a waxen gray tone. This same decoration is used for the large water jug which is cylindrical and has almost no base. Cheese molds, pots, and kettles have a very elementary carved decoration and are not polished. This pottery gives the impression, for its forms, decoration and black color,

of archeological pieces, which is not strange, because historians say that this technique of smoking was used by Celtic potters of the northwest. The potter of Llamas, as so many others, has had to make innovations in his production, with relative success, as the traditional utensils are sold much less.

BASQUE COUNTRY-NAVARRE

In this wide area, there is only one potter, in Narvaja, in the province of Alava, who makes wine pitchers and pots for *requesón,* a kind of cottage cheese. Until a few years ago there was another pottery, in Lumbier, which had a large production and supplied the whole region; it no longer exists. In the provinces of Vizcaya and Guipúzcoa, there have been very few potteries, and here we might quote Caro Baroja's statement that "wood and iron are the two great elements in the material Basque culture, in which ceramics, for example, has seldom achieved more than a symbolic value, not as in other areas of the peninsula."

LEON

León still has a significant number of potteries compared to other areas such as Old Castile, where in the recent past

there was a wealth of potteries which has disappeared.
There is an interesting production by women potters in the province of Zamora, where in Moveros, Pereruela, and Carbellino a very primitive technique is still in use. The wheel must be turned by hand and one must kneel in order to work the pieces. The women are the potters in these places and the men help to load the kiln. One not familiar with these pieces might think they are all alike, since they use the same technique and are made in the same region, but this is not so.
The magnificient jug for carrying water, of **Moveros,** is incredibly delicate and its design reminds us of the primitive use of gourds to carry liquids. The forms are accompanied by the golden color of the clay with some darker areas resulting from the fire, like streaks of brownish and grayish tones. All the pottery made here is used for water: *botijos,* jugs with strainers in the mouth, drinking cups, tubs, toys, and chestnut roasters. Truly, this pottery is, for its simplicity, some of the most beautiful of the peninsula, uncontaminated by modern times. One of the pieces, the *botijo,* is ingenuously decorated with heads of birds and flowers in relief; we

110

108   Products ready for market, in a pottery
in Jiménez de Jamuz, León

109   A potter in Moveros, Zamora, throws
a piece on a rudimentary wheel

110   The jug from Moveros, Zamora,
combines the beauty of its form with the
texture of the clay and the effect of the kiln

109

111

112

have been unable to learn whether the decoration is traditional or is an innovation which has been adopted in all the potteries. We believe it originated in some little *botijo* made for a gift, as a unique piece, and, being well-received, was repeated and came to be used on all *botijos*.

Quite different from the production of Moveros is that of **Pereruela**. The clay used is quite heat-resistant and the technique is also that of working the material on a spinning table which is the wheel. The forms are crude and imperfect, as the clay has little plasticity, but they have an ungainly charm of their own. The stewing pans made here are known in and sent to distant areas (Galicia, the Basque Country, and Burgos) as they are renowned for producing tasty dishes. The women potters of this town still make bread ovens a meter in diameter, pots of different sizes, and jewellers' crucibles, as well as wine pitchers,

sometimes enriched with grotesque decoration, and other pieces of "modern" or "artistic" pretensions. In **Carbellino,** only two sisters make fine earthenware jugs for water, crocks, and tubs, made on a higher wheel than in Pereruela and Moveros. The forms, repeated in crocks and pitchers, are rough and simple with arching handles planted high on the body. At first, we thought that the imperfection of these vessels—most of them seem lopsided—was due to the age of the elderly potters, but we have found pieces made over one hundred years ago, when there was greater production in the village, which have the same characteristics. It is as if these pitchers were so modest and austere they had renounced symmetry. In **Jiménez de Jamuz** (León), glazed and unglazed pottery is made. It is famous throughout the area, especially the *botijos.* The utensils made are the usual ones: pots, tubs, and wine and

water pitchers; slender and firm, like the graceful smaller narrow-necked jugs with the two delicate handles reaching down to the body. There are two pieces which have recently brought fame to these potteries: the "trick pitcher", which was rarely made before and surely derives from a model created in the seventeenth century, and the *botijo*-bottle, shaped to resemble a priest.

The province of Salamanca boasts many active potteries of long-standing tradition. Although there is an interesting variety of forms from one place to another, here we shall discuss only the production of **Alba de Tormes,** which is of the most consequence. Here we find all the pieces typical of the pottery of the *charros,* the rural people of Salamanca, especially those used for table service: plates, soup tureens, bowls, water pitchers, and fruit bowls. Also, other articles for household use: pots, stewing

113

114

pans, heaters, chestnut roasters, and toys. All of this fine earthenware is glazed and decorated with stylized plant motifs, floral borders, and geometric designs. Names are written in the bottom of bowls, plates and pans. A few years ago there appeared in Alba a new style which does not break with tradition and is very attractive: the "filigree". It is used to crown trick *botijos* (with several spouts) or as a decorative border on ornamenal plates; some pieces reach extraordinary dimensions with the addition of open-work clay which is very reminiscent of Salamanca jewelry. One needs considerable skill to produce this fragile piece of architecture, as the clay must be worked at just the right point of malleability and the potter must allow for the movement of the clay under the effects of the heat.
These decorative articles made in Alba, of a brown-orange color with designs in white clay, appear in many still-life paintings of classical Spanish art, so we can affirm that the forms have not changed.

OLD CASTILE
There are few potteries left in this region, and although some areas were never large producers of pottery, the provinces of Logroño and especially Soria are producers of earthenware today.
Navarrete, in the Rioja region, is an active pottery center with several factories in operation. This is because some have mechanized production of planters, which are sold throughout Spain, while they continue making—on a very small scale—jugs, watering troughs, wine pitchers, and pans, of whitish clay with a yellowish glaze.
In the province of Soria, formerly rich in pottery, the only remaining pottery is in **Tajueco** (Quintana Redonda stopped producing in 1975). The traditional forms have degenerated and the classical pots with lid that were much used in Soria are almost unrecognizable. The *botijos* shaped like Romanesque bell towers and the trick *botijos* still have their traditional charm, glazed halfway down and decorated with light brush strokes of white clay. There is only one family of potters, who had given up their craft to work at gathering resin, and have now come back to making pottery.

ARAGON
A land of Moorish tradition, this is one of the regions that has had the greatest number of potteries.
Later we shall duscuss the earthenware with painting over a tin-based glaze of Arabic tradition. Here we refer to rural production, mentioning those forms which we think have the most personality.
In the province of Saragossa there are two centers which make vessels for

116

water: **Magallón** and **Fuentes de Ebro**,
The forms are similar and in both
places the clay is an unglazed
white-pink. The *botijos,* large casks
transported by cart, spouted pitchers,
small jugs with two handles, planters,
and "penny"-banks are all well-turned
pieces with the roundness of pure,
simple lines and perfectly finished.
In Huesca, the linguistic border with
Catalonia, we find two other pottery
centers with common forms, **Fraga** and
Tamarite de Litera. Curiously, the
pitchers of these two places are similar
to those of Miravet and Venisanet, also
located on the banks of the Ebro, in
the province of Tarragona. The pitchers
of Tamarite have an interesting
decoration painted with manganese
oxide: two very narrow lines and a
stylized border.
Naval, to the north, produces glazed
utensils, interesting for their forms
as well as for the decoration.
Here, traditional forms remain

unadulterated: pitchers with pointed
mouths, shallow, open pots, and
decorated crocks. The decoration
consists of a wavy line of manganese
which blends into the ochre
background. Little pitchers, soup
tureens, and plates have dotted-line
circles of a yellow or greenish color.
And between the Jiloca and Guadalupe
Rivers, dry, hard land where we find
other important pieces of traditional
Spanish pottery: in Daroca, Huesa del
Común and Calanda.
Production in **Daroca** (Saragossa)
ceased a very few years ago, when the
last potter moved to Saragossa (I was
told he went to work as a concierge in
a bank); it consisted of rough water
pitchers, worked on a wheel, with
extraordinary beauty of proportion
and lines. The vessel started from a
narrow base, widened up to the middle,
then began to close in the same
proportion, ending in a narrower neck.
The glazed work, pots and pans, is not
much different from that of Cuenca.
Another distinctive pitcher is made in
Huesa del Común (Teruel). The last
potter had quit working because his
kiln had collapsed and he was working
at farming (growing saffron) since the
market for earthenware utensils was so
diminished it wouldn't have paid him
to fix the kiln. When the first strangers
appeared, interested in his wares, the
situation changed. First he sold his
small stock and then decided to return
to his craft. He now has the kiln fixed.
He makes only jugs, in various sizes,
and little spouted pitchers; the surface,
a rosy white, is wrinkly and has lines
of manganese oxide on the upper part
of the body; the neck is narrow with
two small handles. The result is a
mixture of rustic and delicate which
gives the pieces an archeological charm.
And last, **Calanda,** once an important
center of pottery which supplied the
whole area with immense earthen jars
or casks and large pitchers. All the

*115   The varied production of Jiménez de
Jamuz, León, displayed for sale*

*116   Botijos from Fuentes de Ebro,
Saragossa, set out to dry*

pieces made in Calanda are robust and extraordinarily strong. The clay is a bright red, and the very smooth surface of the vessels is painted with bands of wavy designs in manganese oxide. The huge jars, called *tinajas,* almost a meter high, are decorated with strips of clay along the horizontal seams, which also serve as reinforcement. The two-handled crocks, called *parretas,* usually have a scratched or incised design of dotted circles around the mouth and designs in black on the body.

Until recently there was one potter in Calanda, who died while this book was being prepared. He had been about to quit his craft, because the mine which produced the clay had caved in, and he was also without a kiln. Ten or twelve years ago, the pitchers were sold for 50 pesetas, but then came the domestic tourist in search of drums for Holy Week and film buffs combing the homeland of the great Buñuel, and

117

118

119

117   The dignified jug of Fraga, Huesca

118   A used piece from the pottery of Daroca, Saragossa, no longer in existence

119   Large and small jugs from Huesa del Común, Teruel

120   An example of the variety of botijos *made in Verdú, Lérida*

121   The botijos of Verdú are found even in large cities. Fountain of Canaletas, Barcelona

120

121

they bought and gave new value to the beautiful pottery. The potter decided to continue in spite of the obstacles, and he baked his articles in a relative's tile-kiln. The pitchers and little crocks have lost some of their former quality: their full shapes have been somewhat adulterated, the handles can no longer support the weight of the filled pitchers, the black designs have become blotches. The potter knew that his products were no longer put to their original utilitarian use, but were now "decorative objects". This sad ending gives us pause to question the wisdom of protecting and encouraging artisan production when these products are to be used in a different way than that for which they were originally created.

CATALONIA

In Catalonia there has also been a rich pottery tradition, and though many potteries have disappeared, the rural potters of Catalonia still have a significant production. Here there are no unique forms as we have seen in Aragon, but there are some, such as the *"doll"* of the Ampurdán region, which are peculiar to Catalonia; however, what is truly important is the production of smoked utensils in three towns, two of them in Gerona: Quart and La Bisbal, with similar forms; the other is Verdú, in Lérida.

From the kilns of **Verdú** come chiefly *botijos*. Black *botijos* which are so extensively sold throughout Catalonia and even outside the region, that production is now diversified to include different models for each of the various local markets. There are *botijos* called *"sillons"*, traditionally typical of the fields of Lérida, little jugs with two handles and a spout in the middle of the body, and "standing" *botijos* crowned with a clever handle that closes on itself; others are of more ordinary design, reflecting the tastes of the 1930's.

89

La Bisbal (Gerona) has long been an artisan center and has supplied the whole Ampurdán area for centuries. Mostly glazed earthenware was produced here, for table service and for containing liquids. For many years it has been the Catalonian pottery center with the greatest variety of forms and decorative techniques. At present, the two or three potteries that still make the most traditional, classic pieces of La Bisbal are doing less of this work in favor of dinnerware, coffee sets and sets of beer glasses, which are more profitable.

The decoration of soup tureens, lard crocks, *botijos* in the shape of a ship, cups, and other small pieces consists of spiral designs, flowers drawn with a pattern, a design resembling herringbone, and sailing motifs. The more common pieces are decorated with green smudges on a yellow background, and the *"dolls"* and *botijos* in green.

In La Bisbal, today an important center of industrial ceramics, there is still one artisan who makes smoked pottery: *botijos,* watering troughs for chickens, ovens, small braziers, money-boxes, and an endless assortment of other pieces of pure rural tradition. He shares

122   *There is a large, well-organized production of baking dishes in Breda, Gerona. Baking dishes with unbaked glaze. Breda, Gerona*

123   *Traditional "five sou" plates from Piera, Barcelona*

122

125

124   *Crocks,* botijos, *and large and small jugs from Miravet, Tarragona*

125   *Smoked ceramic pieces from La Bisbal, Gerona*

the market for these items with **Quart**. In two places not far from each other but in different provinces, **Cardedeu** (Barcelona) and **Breda** (Gerona), all the pots and shallow pans used in Catalonia are made. Some, especially the shallow pans, are even exported to the rest of the peninsula. Stewing pots and other pots are used locally; it is hard to find these typically wide, squat pots outside this area.

Miravet (Tarragona), on the banks of the Ebro, is an important center for production of large crocks and tubs of all sizes and types; there is even a square tub for gathering honey. They also make utensils for household use: bowls; *"dolls d'oli"*—oil jars; and glazed *botijos,* with one or several spouts. Articles used to hold water, jugs and pitchers with spouts, are unglazed and shaped like the ones we find farther up the Ebro.

Nearing Castellón we find the first pottery center in this region with no glazed ware, **La Galera** (Tarragona). These pieces are dry, austere, with the beauty of things basic, as we found in Teruel; the forms are the same ones used in neighboring **Traiguera** (Castellón), but more well-turned and of purer lines. The type of jug and

93

126

126   Rabbit hutch, watering troughs, jugs, and water filter from La Galera, Tarragona

127   Typical cup and mortar from La Bisbal, Gerona

128   Different glazes used in La Bisbal, Gerona

129   Pieces in Manises, Valencia, on display for the tourist

130   Graceful little jug from Onda, Castellón, similar to that of Miravet, Tarragona

127

128

129

130

pitcher which appears here belongs to a large family reaching as far as Almería, and is also related, for its oxide decoration, to those of Huesa del Común, Calanda, and Priego (Cuenca).

VALENCIA

The famous fourteenth-century pottery of Manises and Paterna and the eighteenth-century production of the Count of Aranda in Alcora have given universal fame to Valencian ceramics.

Little, if anything, remains of this splendorous past, and we find the

tradition of Alcora only in the potteries of Onda and Ribesalbes.

The production of **Manises** is unrelated to the Spanish Moorish tradition which fell into decadence in the seventeenth century and came under the influence of Alcora when Alcora began making pottery. At present, the Alcora tradition is not followed either. There are very few potteries that have not been modernized, but there are more than 200 industrial factories. Following the popular line of the nineteenth century, there is a pottery in which the Gimeno brothers make worthy and graceful historical "survivals". Other

modest potteries make baroque *botijos* of a very low-brow sort, which would delight Picasso, with that colorist, ornamental Levantine spirit that characterizes one of the areas of Valencian artisanry: toys; and numerous mortars and other kitchen utensils sold throughout Spain.

In **Ribesalbes,** the pottery of the Figás family preserves many models clearly originated in Alcora, since many workers in that factory managed to establish their own potteries during the nineteenth century and they popularized motifs of Alcora pottery. The plates and dishes of fine

La Vall d'Uxó (Castellón) produces pottery for cooking: shallow pans, *"parols"*—pots; chocolate pots, of all sizes. The inside and sometimes part of the outside are glazed, contrasting with the blackened clay. The forms are interesting and all start from a wide base before acquiring the shapes peculiar to each function; these are unrelated to the utensils of Cuenca, Teruel, or Catalonia. Besides the well-known coffee, tea, or beer sets, they make traditional toys—*"obreta"*—sold as far away as Valencia, where they are called *"escuraeta"*, which are miniature reproductions of kitchen ware.

Segorbe, in the mountains of Castellón, produces glazed earthenware for household use and for holding water. The jugs are solid and well-balanced, and in general the forms are robust. The potteries still make a wide variety of pieces, from baking dishes to the *"Virgen de la Cueva"* ("Our Lady of the Cave") *botijos,* with religious figures made with a mold, and including endless pitchers, crocks, and pots for keeping lard.

Other pottery centers, **Alcora, Chiva, Liria,** and **Villar del Arzobispo** (Valencia), produce chiefly green-glazed utensils or water vessels, not particularly distinctive, and of little vitality.

However, **Agost** (Alicante) has more than 18 potteries, which produce casks and *botijos* in white clay—they add salt to it—and the fame of the Agost *botijos* has spread throughout the Levantine region. Forms are very varied and the decorations in relief are harmonious with the forms. The decoration consists of floral designs made in thick liquid ceramic paste, and makes the pieces graceful and attractive. Utensils for use in the fields—jugs, *botijos* so large they are carried by cart, and ordinary *botijos*—are of a classic simplicity.

132

polychromed earthenware, decorated pitchers and basins, and the plates for hanging made by the Figás potter are indeed examples of worthy and well-made artisan work.

In **Onda,** the decorated stannic ceramic work offers simpler models and decorations than in Ribesalbes and the production of *botijos,* pitchers and plates is soon to be lost, as the potteries have been made into factories producing mosaic and decorative tiles. As for pottery in the folk tradition, glazed or unglazed, there are some centers, and we shall mention those with the most distinctive production.

131   *Glazed crocks, jugs, and* botijos *from Segorbe, Castellón, next to* botijos *from Agost, Alicante, in a market*

132   *Cooking ware from potteries of Vall d'Uxó, Castellón*

134

MURCIA

In **Lorca** (Murcia), they make a fine stannic earthenware of lesser quality than that of Onda or Ribesalbes, basic and unconstrained. The tradition of Alcora did not arrive intact to this area, which is close to Andalusian influence: the Lorcan wavy-mouthed pitchers are related to those of Andújar (Jaén) and Triana (Seville), although the decoration is Levantine. The ingenuous designs are scattered asymmetrically. Cups, plates, wine pitchers, and wedding pitchers are made and until recently were sold in all the crockery shops of the region. Now production is sold to tourists at the potteries themselves, and the pieces are used merely for decoration.

In **Totana** and also in Lorca, they make the water jugs used in the region, of beautiful lines, with narrow base and neck and two handles. The very simple decoration consists of overlappiing circular incisions around the body of the jug.

In **Aledo, Mula** and **Peñas de San Pedro** (Albacete), they make the traditional cooking utensils, pots and pans. In Aledo there is an unglazed "spice holder" with three units joined together by flat handles, airy and refined.

In **Chinchilla** and **La Roda** (Albacete) they make glazed pottery with designs in relief of yellowish clay. The most typical pieces are the *"cuervera"*, a pitcher for a type of sangría called *"cuerva"* or *"zurra"*; the *"atascaburras"*, an enormous pot; and spice holders. In Chinchilla, one of the artisans still makes sugar bowls that imitate a basket with a handle, with a nineteenth-century flavor.

Albacete, on the central plateau, is a great producer of wine and there are many places, such as **Tobarra** and **Villarrobledo,** with a tradition of making the immense earthenware casks, called *tinajas,* for storing wine. But the great casks for wine-cellars are no longer made—cement ones are used now—and the *tinajas* that are made are used as planters.

In Villarrobledo, the "jug-making" sisters carry on the tradition of working clay without a wheel, making rough jugs, *tinajas,* well curbs, and tubs used in butchering. They decorate the pieces with a paste of white clay which looks like a bandage wrapped around them, and wavy lines incised with a comb. The combination of these elements and the elementary forms produce an exceptional result.

NEW CASTILE

Another extraordinary pottery is made by the women potters of **La Mota del Cuervo** (Cuenca), worked on a wheel without centrifuge. The artisans must bend over the low wheel. The jugs of Mota are high, slender, with a flat handle that joins the neck to the body. The clay is a grayish yellow color, and

136

137

135   *A row of jugs set out to dry. Totana, Murcia*

136   *Great* tinajas, *casks for wine. Villarobledo, Albacete*

137   *Jug from Villarobledo, Albacete*

when the piece is almost dry, the surface is rubbed with a cloth, giving a polished appearance. They make *tinajas,* small jugs; *"colaores"*—a sort of wide mouthed *tinaja* without a rim; watering troughs, and other pieces for rural use.

Also in Cuenca there is an important center, **Priego,** which produces glazed and unglazed pottery; the glazed ware preserves the forms common to the old production of Cuenca: large jugs for use in the fields, jugs for *aguardiente*—a potent alcoholic beverage; pitchers, and pots. Unglazed vessels for water, of lovely lines, are decorated in red ochre on the upper part of the body. This single-color decoration is related to that of La Galera, Traiguera, Huesa del Común, and Calanda, but here it is more elaborate, with scrolls, bands, and stylizations very reminiscent of the Iberian water vessels.

In the province of Toledo, two towns very near each other have shared the fame for their stannic ceramic work: Puente del Arzobispo and Talavera de la Reina.

On the subject of the history of these potteries and the priority of one over the other, we quote Natacha Seseña: "Because of geographic proximity, likeness of forms and even of the clay, as well as decorative characteristics, the similarity of the work of Talavera and Puente is obvious, and although the Talavera work is more well-known and documented, it is also a fact that the excavations done by Llubiá in 1952, in Puente, uncovered fragments of pieces with the same characteristics as those of its neighboring rival."

But the history of the production of both ceramics has been extensively studied, and the articles of the sixteenth, seventeenth, and eighteenth centuries are catalogued collector items; here we shall briefly discuss present production.

In **Talavera de la Reina** there are several

138

factories, and most of them have been modernized and use industrial glaze. The decoration used in all of them owes to the style that triumphed and gave a fresh impulse to Talavera in the 1930's: pompous and baroque, as dictated by the tastes of a comfortable bourgeoisie who recreated the "Spanish Renaissance" furniture and the popularized imagery of Don Quixote and Sancho. Some factories have tried to get away from this profuse decoration and have recovered old series of past centuries, but these are reproductions, not an unbroken tradition.

Puente del Arzobispo, as we have seen, enjoyed in former eras fame and glory like that of Talavera, But Puente did not commercialize its products as ornamental objects in those crucial years of 1930 to 1940, as Ruiz Luna did. (Ruiz Luna was the potter-artist who, together with Guijo, motivated and designed the series of Talavera

pottery in the early decades of this century.) The plates, bowls, and pitchers, glazed and decorated with greens and yellows, could be bought only fifteen years ago, in all the crockery shops of Madrid, for a mere pittance.

In a few years, production has degenerated from utilitarian and truly "folk" forms, to forms considered more profitable (that is, popular with tourists), and the spontaneous charm of the designs has been lost. Some potteries of the large La Cal family maintain traditional production, but they make articles almost exclusively on order or for sale in their own potteries, which they have turned into stores.

As for rough, unglazed pottery, the classic forms of the region are still made: oval, wide-mouthed jugs, of lovely lines and perfectly turned, small jugs, *botijos,* watering troughs, and money-boxes.

139

140

Villafranca de los Caballeros is another town in Toledo that makes unglazed pottery, of which we shall mention only two pieces: the "snail", which is, or was, used as a megaphone by the crews of reapers, and the small earthenware cricket cages, spherical with myriad little holes. This is not only a toy for children, but reflects many people's taste for the music of crickets singing.

The jugs, watering troughs, and other pieces made here bear a decoration incised with reed combs.

Valdeverdeja (Ciudad Real) and **Cuerva** and **Consuegra** (Toledo) make glazed utensils in the characteristic forms of this rural area. In Cuerva they make decorated jugs called *"ollas majas"*, which have always served as decorative pieces in the kitchens of La Mancha, as part of a woman's belongings. They are placed upside down on the fireplace mantel.

In **Ocaña**, they used to make the immense *tinajas* for keeping wine, but these have been replaced by cement ones made in the wine-cellars. Now, production is limited to smaller casks used as planters, other kinds of planters, jugs, and *botijos.*

In **Navalcarnero** a traditional artisan has begun producing a line of distinctive sculpture, at once ingenuous and complicated. He reproduces Biblical scenes or aspects of the everyday life that surrounds him, composing baroque groupings of people, animals, and objects.

We shall not mention other potteries in this extensive and varied geographic area, because we do not believe their production is of such distinctive personality as to be included in this work which attempts to take in such varied themes.

EXTREMADURA

This region, like its neighbor, Andalusia, is rich in potteries, but we shall single

138   *Jugs from La Mota del Cuervo, Cuenca*

139   *Examples of the production of an excellent artisan of Puente del Arzobispo, Toledo*

140   *The "olla maja", traditional piece of Cuerva, Toledo*

141   *Jugs of Priego, Cuenca, waiting to be fired*

142   *These jugs in Ubeda, Jaén, are being dried in the pottery*

143   *The glazed production of Ubeda, Jaén, and its traditional rooster*

144   *Botijos in "lamido" technique from Salvatierra de los Barros, Badajoz*

103

146

the latter decorated by the technique of "burnishing". There is such a variety of forms in both techniques that this may be considered the most important pottery center of Spain. The glazed earthenware is decorated with white clay and the decoration is like a simpler version of that done in Alba de Tormes (Salamanca). This work is done on all types of pitchers and crocks and small utensils for household use. The shallow pans, pots, and tubs are undecorated and sold only locally.

A special technique is used in the decoration of the wide variety of *botijos* and unglazed water pitchers. The technique is called *"lamido"*, which refers to the effect of being worn shiny with use. It consists of applying a layer of ceramic paste of a darker red over the nearly dry piece. On this layer, designs are made with a rounded stone which gives a polish to the surface it touches. This work is done by women, while throwing the piece on the wheel is exclusively men's work. The decoration is rich and varied, using border designs, floral motifs and stripes.

ANDALUSIA

This is such a wide area and has such a wealth of pottery that we must be more selective. The Arab past, which has solid and deep roots in this region, left an indelible mark on the world of folk arts and crafts among its peoples. In the province of Almería, which borders on the Levantine region, we see the graceful, delicate pottery of **Vera,** today made only by one elderly potter. The undulating forms with thin sides seem humble imitations of palace finery.

Small-mouthed pitchers with a narrow base, globlets, and other articles are made with white, porous clay. The forms are related to those of **Totana** (Murcia) and **Andújar** (Jaén), where they also make pitchers with wavy

145 Glazed production of Lucena, Córdoba

146 Botijos and money-boxes from Montehermoso, Cáceres

out only two types of pottery. We shall merely mention Casatejada, Arroyo de la Luz, Montehermoso, and others in the province of Cáceres; likewise Cabeza del Buey, Trujillo, and Fregenal de la Sierra, in the province of Badajoz. **Ceclavín** (Cáceres) is known in the region for its *"enchinada"* ware, fine earthenware with inlays of small bits of quartz which form outlines of flowers on the body of pots and jugs. This technique is related to that used in Portugal, especially in Nisa in the Upper Alentejo, but the decoration here is less ornate. Both glazed and unglazed ware is made here, and the "Chinese" decoration is used only on special pieces.

In **Salvatierra de los Barros** there is a varied production which reaches a wide market, thanks to the enterprising spirit of wholesalers who, in cooperation with the families of potters, have established themselves in distant areas. Both glazed and unglazed ware is made,

mouths forming four corners. These pieces seem classical, and were the protagonists of the still-life paintings of Zurbarán, a sort of table service somewhere between rustic and refined. In **Níjar,** there was a very popular production of pottery, imperfectly glazed, but with a great freshness of design. These platters and dishes are being made less and less, since the many potters of the lovely town prefer to go bag and baggage with the tourist trade. They believe that the traditional decoration, a blue floral design, marks the articles as utilitarian; they have adopted, almost exclusively, a decoration in bright colors they call "Chinese": a renunciation of a more demanding technique and a concession to a market influenced by a mistaken idea of "modern".

We shall point out only two types of production in the province of Córdoba: the unglazed, used for holding and transporting water, and the glazed utensils of Lucena.

La Rambla is a large pottery producer which supplies all the markets in southern Spain with *botijos.* The clay, white and very porous, is excellent for keeping water cool. The potters of La Rambla are models of creative capacity, for in *botijos* alone there are more than twenty different models: barrel-shaped *botijos,* with rounded body and graceful base, double *botijos* that look like bell towers, etc. These articles, like those of Agost, are decorated in relief with liquid ceramic paste, or with incised circles and lines made with the fingers in the soft clay. Besides *botijos,* they make pitchers, casks, bowls in which *gazpacho* is made, and watering troughs.

Several other places in the province make the same type of articles, among them **Palma del Río, Montilla, Bujalance,** and others.

In speaking of glazed ware, we must mention **Lucena,** also in the province of

147

148

149

150

Córdoba, for here they have kept forms and decorations nearly untouched, and for this it is practically an exception. Lucena, in spite of having only two potteries at present, has a large production with a variety of forms. In the colors used (green, blue, and brownish manganese) these pieces are similar to the most authentic present production of Puente, but not so in the thickness, necessitated by the type of clay used, or the forms. The dishes, platters, and tubs have a wide base and straight sides, which we shall see again in the pottery of Granada. They are glazed inside and out and have a wide mouth. They are made in many sizes, some for keeping small quantities of preserves in the kitchen (lard, olives, or pickled preserves), and others, which can be quite large, for putting up preserves for the year. The small pieces are decorated with a floral border and the larger ones have a design like an olive leaf on the body. All the pieces are decorated in color: mortars, small pots, pitchers, oil jars. The tubs are beautiful and the decoration simple and elegant. We must mention the form and color of the *"perulas"*, one-handled jugs for keeping oil, vinegar, or liquor; they have a rounded body and are decorated with horizontal incisions from the base to the neck. The beautiful green color of these vessels is achieved through tedious manual operations. The color and form of these pieces has remained unchanged for two hundred years, as their presence in many Andalusian still-life paintings testifies. The *tinajas,* not very large, are used for olive oil and have extraordinary lines. They are thrown on a wheel from a small base and end in a mouth with a rim; they are glazed on the inside. In the city of **Granada,** next to the Puerta de Fajalauza, there are several potteries whose origins we might find in Moorish Granada, before the sixteenth century.

147   The delicate forms of pottery from Vera, Almería

148   The production of Palma del Río, Córdoba, is used for containing water

149   Glazed crocks. Lucena, Córdoba

150   The white porous clay keeps water cool. A water-seller's. Seville

111

151

152

151 *Plate from Granada*

152 *Two-tone decoration used in Granada*

153 *A piece typical of Guadix, Granada*

The production of these potteries is traditional, glazed, and decorated with heavy brush strokes in blue and green. The forms of the dishes, platters, and tubs are similar to those of Lucena we have already described. The pitchers take on different shapes: some are rounded with wide mouths, others have straight sides like vinegar cruets. There are both glazed and unglazed water jugs, although nowadays the demand is for glazed ones for decorative purposes. There are still traditional potters who make articles for household and farm use, such as milking pails, crocks, and tubs, while the larger potteries with greater production make a wide variety of decorative plates, ornamental pitchers with baroque designs in blue and green, ash trays, flower vases, and other pieces not belonging to the traditional pottery of Granada which was distributed and used throughout southern Spain, with the characteristic motifs of the pomegranate, flower, and star, intricately drawn.

Also in the province of Granada, we must mention the unglazed earthenware of **Guadix,** which is of a bright red and an unusual plasticity. Here they make *botijos,* including large ones with two handles; pitchers and jugs with rounded bodies; *botijos* in the shape of a rooster; goblets with lids and decorated with harmonious groupings of birds and flowers, fashioned by hand. The goblet is a nineteenth-century style piece of rare charm and highly valued, but making it is a slow process as the different parts must be baked separately, and it is very fragile. The production of other towns in Granada, such as **Cuéllar de Baza** and **Huéscar,** also has beautiful lines, but lacks the distinctiveness of the red clay of Guadix.

In **Seville,** the production of the district of Triana is on the verge of

153

"fine earthenware" dishes, platters, and large pans have a streaked decoration. The effect of the colors dripped on the dark clay is very pretty, and we have found no other pottery on the peninsula which gets such lovely results with this technique.

In Jaén, **Ubeda** is a fairly well-known pottery center because some of the artisans have succeeded in improving the glaze so that the traditional pieces have a more "refined" appearance and so are more attractive to the public looking for "decorative pieces". One artisan, named Tito, has gone back to making the larger pieces, which had been abandoned: large jugs for use in the fields and large containers for olive oil. He also makes a series of refined plates for hanging, with incised decoration, for a city-dwelling public. At the same time, another pottery continues making large unglazed jugs and the classic platters and bowls, decorated with ingenuous, rude swirls and animal or floral designs, destined for sale in crockery shops.

Last, and leaving many potteries unmentioned, we shall cite **Andújar**, related to Vera and Triana in the wavy shape of the mouths of the pitchers. At present, however, characteristic production is fine, white, glazed ware with design in blue. The multicolored decoration used for some time has been completely abandoned; at most, there may be flecks of yellow alongside the blue brush strokes. A curious piece made only here is the "grotesque pitcher", which has three bodies and is decorated with figures molded by hand, as in Guadix, of birds and angels. Some, since the Napoleonic invasion, have included little human heads representing French soldiers. Here they also make musical pipes in the shapes of little mules carrying water jars, bulls, and two types of human figures. One of the latter wears a sort of Phrygian cap and the other, a *picador's* hat, with

disappearing. The growth of the city has displaced the kilns; the potters have found no help in keeping their traditional potteries. So, in a few years, the production of Triana will be finished forever: its fine glazed earthenware and its popular production of butchering tubs, smaller tubs, bowls, pitchers, jugs and planters, all decorated in attractive polychrome work, always of animals related to hunting, older and more painstakingly made, and swirls and diamond shapes painted with a fine brush. Nor will there be the charming inscriptions in relief on the houses of Seville, because the production of some

of the most important potteries is being replaced by others done with industrial glaze and without the handmade mold. In the province there are many potteries that make fine earthenware water vessels. Worth mentioning are the jugs of **Lebrija**, with a high neck and small base.

As for the provinces of Málaga, Cádiz, and Huelva, we shall mention only one town of the latter, **Cortegana**, where glazed earthenware for cooking is made, including the familiar pots with two handles, pans, and little pitchers, glazed on the inside and with a touch of glaze dripped on the outside. The

154

155

154 *Collection of plates and serving dishes from Cortegana, Huelva*

155 *Glazed kitchen ware and small, unglazed jugs. Cortegana, Huelva*

156 *Traditional decoration. Triana, Seville*

157 *The "grotesque pitcher". Andújar, Jaén*

156

114

low crown and wide brim. The pipes are glazed with a painted blue design, or painted with bright colors after baking; the latter are the most popular and are sold at fairs and *romerías* (pilgrimages). Both Andújar and neighboring Arjonilla make miniature reproductions of flower vases, pitchers, spice-holders, holy-water basins, *botijos,* etc., which are made like regular earthenware pieces.

BALEARIC ISLANDS

Historically, the island of Majorca has been the most important pottery center, and it still is. There is only one potter working in Minorca, in **Ciutadella**, but his is a limited line, and inspired by the Majorcan forms. The same occurs in **Ibiza,** although one potter, who signs himself "Daifa", makes imaginative and ingenuous figures approaching *"siurells"* and the Carthaginian pieces of the archeological museum, all of them touched by his imagination. Another potter, a native of the peninsula who has moved to Ibiza, makes simple, dignified stylizations of the votive figures in the museum, which are well received by the summer tourist market. These are examples of the ability to create "new folk art", but it is hard to maintain an equilibrium as the market is undiscriminating.

On the island of Majorca there are several pottery centers; we shall mention **Inca**, which has several potteries in operation. Their glazed pottery includes almost all the household pieces used today: dishes, platters, *"amb orelletes"* soup dishes; they also make unglazed ware. The platters and large dishes are decorated with white clay and simple patterns. Some of the unglazed pieces have the typical Mediterranean shapes, such as the jug with the rounded body, two handles, and long neck. The large jars, crocks, pans, canteens, and other

157

158   The Majorcan jug is a favorite throughout the Balearic Islands

159   Detail of the modeling of the clay whistles called "siurells" in Catalan

160   Clay whistle. Sa Cabaneta, Balearic Islands

vessels are still made in the potteries of the city of Palma, and in Inca, **Pórtol**, and **Cabaneta**.

The small, rough imitations of the gracile little jugs of **Felanitx**, which were ornamental objects heavily decorated and with open work, are made with varying degrees of success. Some, such as those of **Consell**, have evolved into little baskets decorated with ceramic paste similar to those made in Manises.

Interesting ceramic items are the musical pipes variously called *"siurells"*, *"xiurells"*, or *"siulets"*, which, although they will be described in the section on toys, deserve special mention here because the antecedents to these whistles were found, quite by accident, in a Moorish pottery of the Almoravid dynasty of the twelfth or thirteenth century in Palma. Quoting G. Roselló Borday, we can say that these little figures fashioned from clay, bearing intentional fingerprints, have their precedent in the "study of these little figures found in a digging of reasonably certain chronology which enables us to date with some accuracy the two examples of Majorcan ceramic toys, though they do not have a whistle. Doubtless, they are of the Muslim period, as the rest of the findings, and there are not sufficient reasons to suppose that they are of peninsular origin, as the site of the dig was a pottery".

CANARY ISLANDS

While the peninsula has always exported pottery and clay material for construction to the Canaries, on all the islands there is still production of earthenware derived directly from the native culture, whose forms and techniques still survive. It is obvious that this production is more primitive than that of the earliest potteries of the peninsula: it is done only by women, who work the clay without a wheel, modeling the pieces on a thin, flat stone. The pieces, water jugs, corn roasters, ovens, pitchers, incense burners, and receptacles for kneading corn meal, are unglazed.

On Great Canary Island, there are only three potteries. One is in **Atalaya de Santa Brígida**, where the potter who best preserves the tradition is Francisco Rodríguez—odd, since most of the potters are women. He decorates his water jugs and pitchers with incised designs, and makes extraordinarily primitive animal figures.

In a district of Gáldar, called **Hoya de Pineda** (the name refers to its being tucked in between two hills), there is only one potter, a woman, left. Her pieces are beautiful and, in spite of her advanced age, she still makes very large pieces such as corn roasters, which are 60 to 70 centimeters wide. She explains that, besides making and baking the pieces, she used to take them by donkey to sell in other villages. The pieces are covered with bright red ochre, and over this layer she makes designs with a stone while the clay is still soft. Sometimes the designs are vertical, other times like a border encircling the piece. To the jugs and pitchers she adds little handles, and projections that serve as handles which are also found in Moroccan and Algerian pottery in the Berber region. The potter of **Los Lugarejos** now works in a sort of private museum—Cho Zacarías—in San Mateo, which has a beautiful collection of pieces of Great Canary pottery. He learned pottery from a blind woman potter in Los Lugarejos, but his products are now very adulterated, as he seeks inspiration in the prehispanic forms he finds in scientific publications.

In Tenerife, only **La Victoria de Acentejo** still produces pottery, although the islands used to have such important pottery centers as San Andrés which produced so many articles sold in Lanzarote and Fuerteventura that it is still known as San Andrés de las Ollas (St. Andrew of the Pots). The potter of La Victoria is an older woman who does all the work herself: making the pieces, drying, baking. The wide variety of forms includes items from coffee roasters to crocks, pitchers, pots, and braziers. On the island of La Gomera, the only place pottery is made is in **Chipude**, where the same method we have seen in native potteries of the other islands is used. Here the forms, also unglazed and covered with red ochre which is then polished, are squatter and the sides are thick. Now miniature replicas of the commonly used vessels are made for tourists to buy as souvenirs.

161   Splendid form of the pottery of Chipude, Gomera

161

metalwork

The art of working metal is one of the oldest industries, accompanying western man throughout his historical process. From the first weapons of copper, followed by utensils of bronze and then iron, up to the recent steel industry, the techniques of working and casting metals have provided man with all manner of articles: instruments for attack and defense, tools for his trades and industries, symbols of power and wealth, ornate forms and household utensils.

All this complex world of necessary artifacts which surrounded the individual throughout his life, based on the almost magical properties of the metals, malleability and hardness, has been replaced by the qualities of the new materials of the technological revolution and new modes of production. Thus, these ancient industries have fallen into complete decadence in our culture and, if any remain, it is due more to the decorative aspect of the objects than to any direct use.

162   Wrought-iron insignia of barber shop with brass basins. Argamasilla de Alba, Ciudad Real

163, 164, 165, 166   Process of melting in a foundry in Lucena, Córdoba
Casting the iron. The liquid metal is poured through the holes to fill the mold. Once cooled, the pieces are removed

162

168

169

*167   Beautiful, traditional copper kettle
from the best master craftsmen of Guadalupe,
Toledo*

*168, 169   Two traditional copper pieces, jug
and chocolate pot, with repoussé brass lid.
Guadalupe, Toledo*

WORK IN COPPER, BRONZE, AND BRASS

It seems likely that it was the Arabs who introduced these metals to the peninsula. They were used exclusively for household utensils and ornaments, and the traditional work of artisans has continued in this line.

Until the beginning of the twentieth century, all important towns and villages had a master coppersmith who supplied the area with cauldrons, pots, braziers, chocolate pots, and measuring utensils for liquids and grains. With a thin sheet of this reddish material, the coppermith's hands, ingenuity, and good taste created beautiful forms by hammering the malleable material on a small anvil between his legs. We find rounded *botijos,* open kettles, warming-pans with lids with incised or hammered decoration, and an endless variety of household utensils. Now these pieces belong to the world of antiques, along with the old glazed ceramics or traditional furniture. These utilitarian pieces are still made in the centers where the tradition was kept alive, but now they have other uses. In **Guadalupe** (Toledo), the whole town works at "beating" the copper, and they produce an infinity of articles, for there is still the tradition of a bride's providing chocolate pots and kettles for her new home.

In all of Andalusia, but especially in the Gypsy communities of **Granada** and **Córdoba**, copper and brass are worked. The pieces have become smaller and smaller in response to the heavy tourist trade which cannot buy large, cumbersome pieces. Now they are merely souvenirs of no interest. In the province of Salamanca, in the town of **Navafría**, there is a coppersmith's shop where copper is cast and wrought using the old method of the traditional forge, with the drop-hammer powered by the hydraulic power of the Cega River.

Also in the city of **Albacete** there is still a coppersmith's shop, owned by a family from Chinchilla, which makes saucepans, kettles, cooking pots, and candlesticks, and restores and mends old pieces. In **Riópar**, also in Albacete, there is an important industry, begun in the eighteenth century for the exploitation of the zinc mines. Its production consists of the artisan crafts of casting and chiseling bronze religious iconography, candelabra, and kettles, saucepans and braziers; and copper chocolate pots and pitchers called *"jarros de San Juan"*. In **Valverde del Camino** (Huelva), where there is a great tradition of copper and brass, the process has been partially mechanized, with unfortunate results. At the same time they worked with copper, our traditional rural and urban coppersmiths also made pieces of brass, a yellow alloy of copper and zinc, with which they cast mortars, trivets, heaters, and five- or six-armed candelabra.

170

171

There is still significant production of brass items in **Lucena** (Córdoba), where they make beautiful oil lamps in the traditional design with small screens of a Renaissance cut, to be used for decoration.

We find it interesting that copper and brass articles are not appreciably different from one area to another. Aside from small artisan industries (with all the folk flavor and designs in cast bronze for use on furniture or in religious iconography, which is made in **Mijas,** in Málaga, and in **Jaén,** as well as in Riópar) there is only the casting of bells. In Galicia, there are modest

foundries that make bells which fill the limited rural needs: bells for rural parishes, cowbells, and bells for adorning animals' headgear. In Vitoria and Madrid, large industries monopolize the casting of bells, which are exported. Iron and tin are alloyed and cast at a temperature of 1000 ° C. in molds which must then be broken. These sonorous bells are heard throughout the towns of Spain and South America.

IRON WORK

Since long ago, the arts of the iron forge have enjoyed great prestige; in the

era of Roman domination, there was praise for the weapons forged by the Celto-Iberian people with minerals extracted from the Hispanic subsoil. In the late thirteenth century there were notable nuclei of blacksmiths in the Basque Country-Navarre area, and in Catalonia, Cuenca and Toledo, surely a continuation of a profound pre-Roman tradition.

At the end of the Gothic period and during the Renaissance, we find some cultured, artistic creations in wrought iron, of great value: iron grates, balconies, knockers, weather-vanes, braziers, locks for chests of drawers,

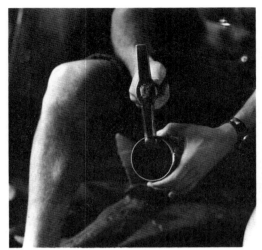

172

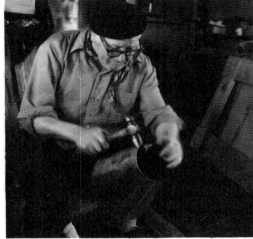

173

170   Decorative brass olive-oil lamp, with a
stereotyped ornamentation reflecting
"cultured" tastes. Lucena, Córdoba

171   Oil lamp. Lucena, Córdoba

172, 173   Master coppersmiths hammering
the pieces of copper into desired form.
Guadalupe, Toledo

174   Beautiful wrought-iron grille. Cau
Ferrat Museum, Sitges, Barcelona

174

125

of which there is a beautiful collection
in the Cau Ferrat Museum in Sitges.
This art, although it becomes distanced
from its upper-class origins, continued
to be practiced in the seventeenth and
eighteenth centuries, as we see in
wrought iron grates and balconies,
andirons, pot-hangers, and other
household utensils, although they may
be the work of rural craftsmen.
Thus we can distinguish, beginning in
the nineteenth century, some centers of
interesting popular-level iron work, each
with its own distinctive characteristics.
The iron work of Extremadura reaches
to Andalusia and is characterized by
the use of arabesques alternating with
animal silhouettes, as we see in door-
knockers, racks for hanging utensils,
legs of roasting spits, and in the
graceful grates, lanterns, and iron gates
typical of the architecture.
The iron work of Aragon used Moorish
decoration and is characterized by the
vigorous structure of the grates, torches,
or lamps for burning candlewood.
The production of the Basque Country-
Navarre area includes objects for the
central fireplace kept under the
bell-shaped funnel of the chimney,
which was the most important piece in
the home. In some villages of this area
one can still find the monumental and
artistic andirons, incorporating
candlesticks and with a crosspiece
which supports the pot-hangers, and
surrounded by storage for pots.
Catalonia and the Pyrenees area have an
abundant production of articles for the
hearth, especially the chains used to
hang pots or kettles over the fire; these
are complicated and require prodigious
forge work as they are made of several
chains beautifully twisted. The
andirons, however, are smaller. And as
we move south to the Ebro, where the
kitchen is no longer the center of
family life, simple tripods fulfill all the
kitchen needs, holding the pot or kettle
over the fire.

175

176

177

The art of making these articles has been lost, although we still see them being used in small villages. Today's rural blacksmith has no specific function—nor did he in centuries past, as he also acted as locksmith, making locks and keys; as maker of lattices, grates, and balconies; as cutler; and he shod horses and made nails and even anvils. Today he has less and less work; traditional architecture is being abandoned, cutlery is centralized in a few places in the peninsula, work animals are being replaced by machinery, nails are made industrially, anvils are no longer needed, and tools are sold everywhere by large firms. There is little room in this new way of life for a profession that was once essential and was the first to be recognized as rendering a public service.

The blacksmiths we have found mostly do "mending" and are even beginning to call themselves "mechanics", since they repair tractor ploughs...

In some local smithies in Albacete, Andalusia, Badajoz and Galicia, they still make beautiful farming implements: spades, hoes, pitchforks, and rakes, each having the forms peculiar to the area where it is made, in wrought iron or steel. It wider markets, implements of cast iron have appeared. It is interesting that tools so close to men show such variety in the form of the tool itself, the thickness of the handle, the degree of roughness or refinement.

In some southern areas where traditional architecture still prevails, as in La Mancha, Andalusia, and Extremadura, iron-work grates and lattices are still made. Other areas, where the rural population is moving to the cities, have no need for these articles, as there is scarcely any construction being done.

In some places, the tradition of iron work has been preserved, almost by chance, by finding a market for

175   Coarse central "cremall" and other iron pieces in a Catalonian kitchen, wrought by local blacksmiths

176   Local blacksmiths also made tools for working the land

177   Interior of a blacksmith's shop. Minglanilla, Cuenca

178, 179   Different kinds of sickles for use in different jobs or in different areas

180   Process of finishing sickles. La Solana, Ciudad Real

181   A peasant stops his work to sharpen the ancestral scythe. Balaguer, Lérida

178

179

180

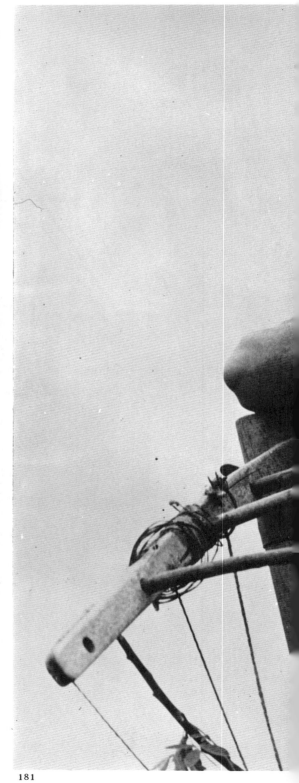

181

decorative objects: La Debla de los Navalmorales (Toledo), no longer in operation, and **Albarracín** (Teruel). The creative capacity and imagination of the local blacksmiths has succeeded in maintaining a line of well-made decorative objects while abiding by all the rules of tradition.

Cutlery has become concentrated in **Albacete**, where there already was a long-standing tradition and some shops still specialize in artisan cutlery such as pocket and hunting knives. They use steel from Bilbao and the handles are made of bull horns or deer feet. In **Madrigueras**, also in Albacete, cutlery is also made, but here the process is highly mechanized; the same is true of **Santa Cruz de Mudela** (Ciudad Real). The knives made in Galicia are different, truly of folk craft, unpresuming and not commercialized. In **Lugo**, they have stained wooden handles with burned-in designs. In the Canary Islands there are curious knives

182   Peddler of penknives and hunting knives. Albacete

183   Arsenal of tools used by the backsmith

182

130

185

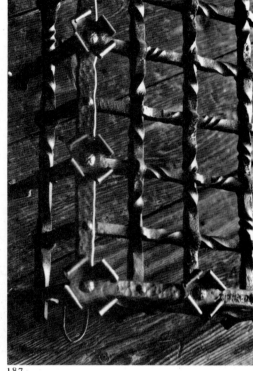

187

186

184   *Tin-plate version of sumptuous Muslim lamps of brass*

185   *Collection of door handles and knockers made by the artisan blacksmith of Albarracín, Teruel*

186   *The production of pocket knives in Albacete reaches markets throughout Spain*

187   *Beautiful grille work done recently in Albarracín, Teruel*

133

188

189

190

with rounded handles full of decorative inlays; their origin is unknown, as they are quite different from anything found on the peninsula.

Sickles, scythes, long, narrow razors, a kind of sickle with a hooked point, and a whole series of cutting instruments are made in **La Solana** (Ciudad Real) with the traditional forms and rudimentary methods. And yet, machetes and other cutting instruments are exported to Morocco, Turkey, and Cuba. These articles are also made in **Bienservida** (Albacete) where the forge still uses a great hand-operated bellows.

In the Basque Country-Navarre area they also make hatchets, especially in **Leiza,** where they make the traditional Navarran convex-shaped hatchet, and the straight-cut ones of Biscay.

Steelyards, ancient means of weighing, are still being made by Galician blacksmiths, as they are still the preferred measuring device in local markets. They are also made in **Madrigueras** (Albacete), where they are forged in iron and in stainless steel and have a hanging ball; this town has been known for years as *"romanero",* "maker of steelyards".

191

WORK IN TIN PLATE

This more modern metal, which is worked in thin sheets, a bit as if it were cardboard, and using the technique of folding, cutting, and piercing, has been used to make beautiful, modest specimens of popular ornaments. Violant i Simorra believes that its use came from neighboring France, but we can affirm that it was greatly developed in Extremadura and Andalusia from where it reached the New World, especially Mexico, where there is a rich and creative use of this ductile, inexpensive, and shiny material. On the popular altars of the peninsula, especially in the south, we find delicate flower vases made of this material, which the local artisan has painted with bright colors. The material, which, as we have said, is easily worked, is made into ingenuous, colorful, and baroque objects which are imitations of the more difficult filigree work done with other materials.

188, 189   Interior of a workshop in Madrigueras, Albacete, where scales and steelyards are made

190   Beautiful scales in use

191   Vase of tin plate, inspired by the traditional vases in churches. Granada

192

193

194

Tin plate is an inexpensive material which can be made into beautiful and brilliant objects, such as the indoor lanterns used in Andalusia, decorative candelabra used in popular masses, mirror frames and an infinity of popular-level "luxury" items.
Another area of use is in utensils for cooking and in shops: cans for keeping olive oil, candlesticks, cruets, gelatin and cake molds, milk pails, oil measures, and many other articles. These things are still made throughout Spain, in Granada, Toledo, Madrid, Extremadura, Murcia, and Catalonia. But the rising cost of labor has meant that, in the last twenty years, they have been disappearing from the market; although the inexpensive material made them economical, and therefore popular, they require many hours of work. This material has ample possibilities and decoration in open work or piercing can produce a great richness of design, especially when it plays with

the subtle effects of light through the holes. This aspect has been exploited, what with the "decorative" trends motivated by tourism, giving birth to a series of decorative objects, trite and usually not requiring any expertise on the part of the craftsman.

TIN CASTING
This metal, used for many centuries for ornaments and tableware, had fallen into total disuse in Spain. A European trend, especially in Italy, bringing back this metal, a popular imitation of luxurious silver dinnerware, has given impulse to the making of "historical" reproductions of articles made of tin.
In **Pedraza de la Sierra** (Segovia), there is a shop which casts and polishes archaic jugs, platters, goblets, and many other utensils, which have only a decorative function. The work is welldone and the designs, splendid; but this is historical reproduction, not unbroken tradition.

192, 193, 194   Lamps of recent production using traditional forms with varying degrees of success, intended for decorative use. Granada

195   Interior of a workshop. Barcelona

136

196

196   Humble utensils with the simple grace of uncluttered forms

197   Tin-plate articles are rarely sold in the cities these days

197

138

leatherwork

198

Spain has always been a nation of livestock raising, with a great tradition of tanning and working animal hides. The leather industry is of Arab influence and the leatherwork of southern Spain enjoyed great fame throughout Europe during the Middle Ages. Especially famous were the "Cordovans" and gilt or printed leather which are refined, sumptuous crafts, principally of Moorish tradition. Also most likely of Moorish origin is the tradition of richly adorned beasts of draught, mounts, and pack animals, with work in leather, tacks, tassels, and pompons. This popular custom common to the eastern and southern regions reached the northern areas, according to Violant i Simorra, in about the seventeenth century, and was strongly developed there due to travel and the commercial traffic in these areas, preserving a showy, lively popular nature. Here we shall discuss, then, the noble profession of harness-making, no longer widely practiced; and the beautiful works in leather which the popular tradition of belt-making has developed.

Harness-making
This is a rich and complex craft which includes everything from working with

198 Rural workshop where horse-collars are made. Montehermoso, Cáceres

199 Horse-collars and saddles in the entry of a rural home

199

201

202

the hide, to adorning the pieces with tacks, leather cut-outs, stitchery, tassels, braids, and fringe, to cushioning pack-saddles.

The harnesses differ according to the work the animals do. There are harnesses for pulling carts or coaches, for mounts, for beasts of burden, and for animals that work in the fields. There is also a distinction between harnesses for work and for "dress"; we should remember that the trappings of a horse were a function of the owner's social position.

Beasts of draught. The harnesses of these animals are made of black or light cowhide, and the pieces comprising these trappings are: halter, collar or breast-leather, usually decorated with bells, hanger, buckle covers, crupper, hames, and bags.

During the last century and the early part of this century, ordinary transportation between cities was by coaches drawn by teams of horses or mules, and the carrier adorned the whole team with festive trappings for the end of a trip, or when he entered an important town on his route. The work on these harnesses was done with superimposed leather cutouts, tacks combining various designs of floral or geometric inspiration, silk and woolen fringes and pompons, and adornments of badger hair. There is a lovely collection in the Fomento de Obras y Construcciones in Barcelona, made in the early twentieth century and used by a Barcelona company which covered the Saragossa-Madrid-Valladolid route. Besides decking out the animals, they also adorned the windshields of the coaches, and in rural Tarragona, one can still see coaches with delicate designs in leather cut-outs and the owner's initials.

In all the agriculturally rich areas there are old harness-makers who can still do the work of years gone by, but they have been reduced to repairing old

200   The cheerful, humble trappings of a village burro

201   Leather and metal tacks are used to achieve beautiful ornamental effects

202   Beautiful trappings—reminiscent of medieval equine fashions—of a horse in Tomelloso, Ciudad Real

203

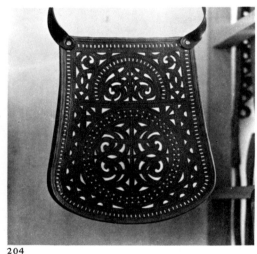
204

harnesses or making ordinary, undecorated harnesses, as the use of beasts of draught is practically non-existent.

In **Los Yébenes** (Toledo), famous for the quality harnesses once made there, they now make articles for hunting and fishing.

Trappings for mounts. Saddles and bridles for mounts, less ornate and more refined, are made in **Huelva** and **Seville**, in Andalusia; in **La Roda** and **Socovos** in Albacete; in the city of **Madrid** and in **Talavera de la Reina**, where they also make the exquisite bridles used by mounted bullfighters.

Harnesses for beasts of burden. This method of carrying weight on the backs of animals is very common in Spain, where there is much difficult, mountainous terrain. A constant traffic of teams of animals transported all kinds of merchandise between towns and villages until a very few years ago; so we find harnesses for pack-animals everywhere, although they are now made more simply, as they are used only for work in the fields.

The components of the trappings of these animals are different from those of beasts of draught, especially in those pieces which protect the animal's back

203 Cutting thin strips of leather

204 Leather bag with cut-out design. Los Yébenes, Toledo

205 Saddle and assorted trappings in a livestock market

206 Beautiful adornment in the Moorish tradition for beasts of burden. Baeza, Jaén

207 The harness-maker applies the traditional decorations to the canvas

205

from chafing and shifting of the load. There is a decorated bridle; the cushioned pack-saddle secured by the girth, and then four layers of cloth or blankets: first a loose cloth, then another, fringed, one, then a long cloth reaching to the crupper, and a final layer over all.

In these trappings, little leather is used; they are mostly made of durable canvas or sailcloth. The sailcloth is industrially made but with traditional designs and colors. Narrow cloth is used for girths and in the cloths worn over the animal's back, covering the cushioned pack-saddle, which is also made of cloth. The crupper, which is looped under the animal's tail and holds tight the cushioning, is usually heavily decorated. It was the city of Burgos, with six shops with vertical looms, that supplied woolen cruppers with simple geometric designs to the whole peninsula (B. Aitken, 1930). At present, the best makers of trappings for beasts of burden still make lovely and colorful halters, decorated with stitchery, with a variety of designs done in wool: stars enclosed in circles over golden buttons, flowers, and geometrical designs. The best-worked pieces come from the mountains

206

207

209

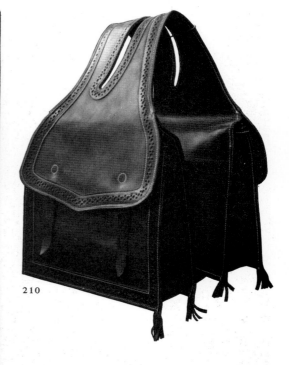

210

of Granada, in **Cadiar** and **Capileira**, in the Alpujarra region; from **Baeza, La Carolina,** and **Andújar** (Jaén); from the cities of **Almería** and **Granada**, and also from **Mérida** (Badajoz).
In the northern regions, León, Galicia, Asturias, and the Basque Country, where oxen are used as beasts of draught and for work in the fields, they make halters of leather and felt, adorned with tacks and pompons of wool, placed over the forehead of the work oxen.

Belt-making
Here, we use belt-making to refer to all leatherwork not used for animals.

The Spanish word for belt-making, *talabartería,* originally referred to making sword-belts *(talabartes)*.
We have already mentioned that in Los Yébenes, the harness-makers of years past now make game-bags, knapsacks, shepherds' leggings, pocketbooks, cartridge belts, and chaps, aprons divided at the lower part and tied behind the thighs and waist, worn by cowherds and other rural folk to protect their clothing while working on horseback. Many of these articles are adorned with borders of tooled designs or designs made with a heated die, or openwork designs of one color over another.

208   *Beautiful festive headstall. Baeza, Jaén*

209   *Skillfully made chaps with incised designs and leather fringe. Los Yébenes, Toledo*

210   *Double leather bag*

211

They also make game-bags, belts with cast metal buckles, the same as used for girths, feed-bags, and simple halters of leather in **Almansa, Elche de la Sierra, Munera,** and other towns in Albacete; in **Arévalo** (Avila) and in **Malpartida** and **Plasencia** (Cáceres), where they have specialized in very pretty billfolds and change purses, within the traditional lines, with cut-out leather. In **Urda** (Toledo) they make the "Manchegan" tobacco pouches for fine-cut tobacco.

In Zamora they make feed-bags, shepherds' bags to be worn slung over the shoulder, very much like the ones the shepherds used to make themselves. More refined articles are made in **Ubrique,** in the province of Cádiz, where skins have always been tanned and made into leather carrying cases and tobacco pouches, dyed with saffron, and used in rural areas. Now the industry has been transformed and makes tobacco pouches and cigarette cases exported to countries around the world. Also in the mountains of Cádiz, and in other towns of Seville and Huelva, they make beautiful chaps of the sort made in Los Yébenes, which are used in Andalusia and Extremadura more than anywhere else.

211   Old leather shepherd's bags and game bags

212   Leather tobacco pouches, coin purses, and billfolds with open-work design. Malpartida, Cáceres

148

214

215

216

213   Interior of a shop where tobacco pouches are made in Ubrique, Cádiz

214   Molds and tools for making cigar cases

215, 216   Two fine examples of well-cured and well-worked leather. Ubrique, Cádiz

217

217 Present-day knapsack modeled on a traditional shepherd's pack

218 Peasant of Toledo with his knapsack

218

wood

We shall begin by talking about the humble articles of wood made by old shepherds or by rural folk who in their spare time do wood carvings, incorporating traditional decorative elements.

We are not referring to the ancient pastoral culture, common to all European peoples, which produced the beautiful examples of work in wood, horn, and leather that we find in museums, and which constitute a true ornamental art of prehistoric tradition; the ways of life that maintained this tradition have completely disappeared, at least as a social group. However, in this same line, we still find occasional works of unquestionable beauty, such as the mortars with openwork base and deeply carved designs, and the carved bowls made by an old shepherd in **Valverde de la Vera** (Cáceres); the crudely carved mortars sold in a *madreñería* (store that sells articles made of wood) in León, made by a ninety-year-old shepherd; and the carved spoons, castanets, and mortars, all beautifully worked, which we find in **Lucillo** (León). To these we must add the beautifully executed carved pieces on exhibit in the Museo de Artes y Costumbres Populares (Museum of Folk Arts and Customs) in Seville, bearing the carved date 1971. Although their origin is not mentioned, they are displayed alongside embroidery from the mountains of Cádiz.

219

219   Wooden case for the whetstone used to sharpen the scythe, made by an old shepherd with simple incised decoration

220   A lathed mortar to which the shepherd has applied a floral decoration. A sculpted mortar with geometric design

221   The use of wooden eating utensils, either lathed or carved, is still frequent

220

154

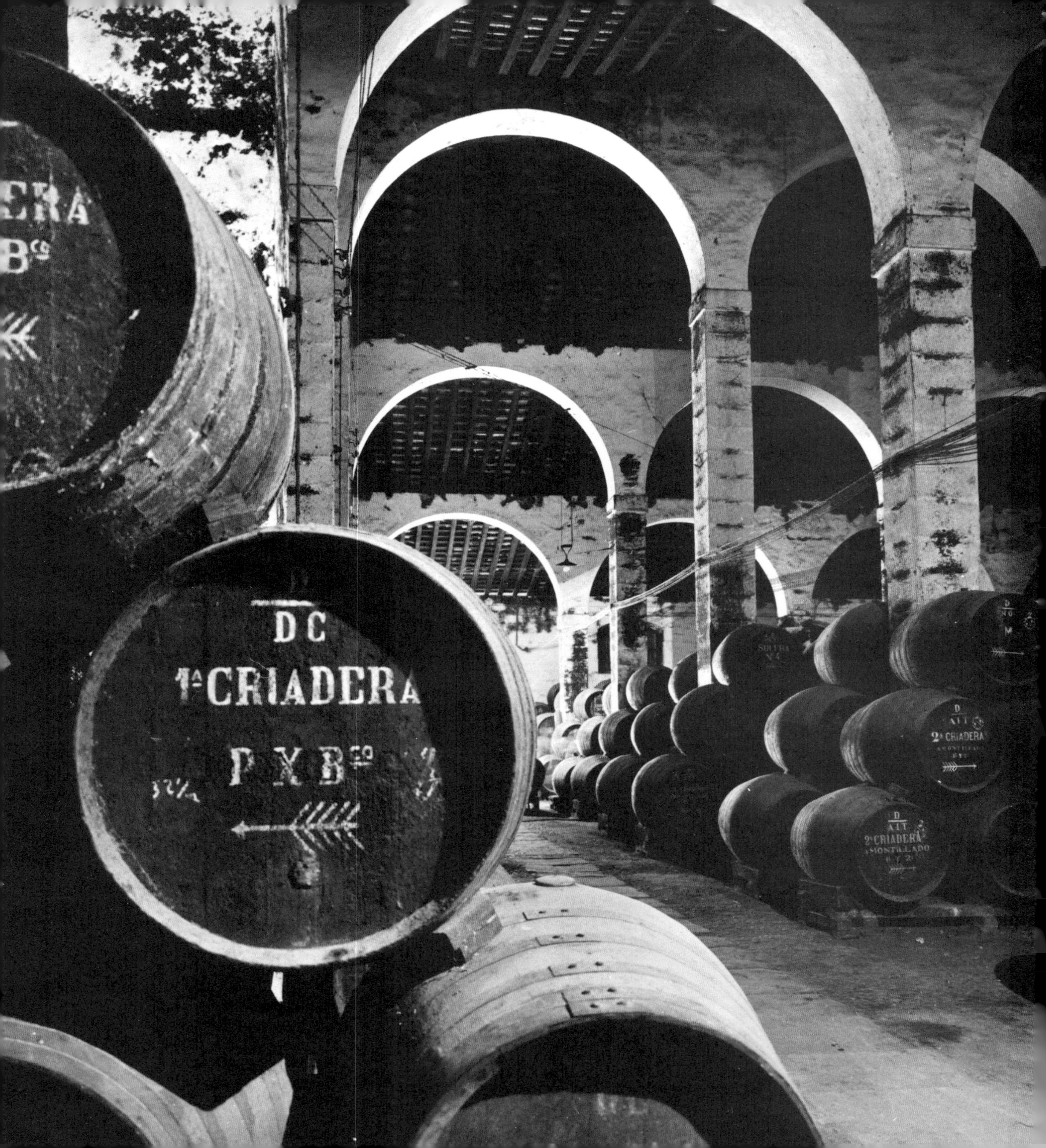
DC
1ª CRIADERA
2ª CRIADERA
AMONTILLADO

223

In several places, they still make knives, forks, and spoons, carved in boxwood, for household use, or to be taken to local markets for sale. We have found some very well made ones in Galician markets, in **Santos de Maimona** (Badajoz), in **Berga** (Barcelona), and in **Tartellá (Gerona)**.

Farming implements

Galicia, a richly wooded region, has kept alive the cooper's trade, here meaning assembling sections of wood to create large curved shapes; it is a way of working with wood that puts wood in competition with pottery, but with a great limitation as to form. In **Betanzos**, they still make large wooden jugs for carrying liquids, in beautiful teak or chestnut, as these woods are among the most water-resistant; pails for both household use (washing) and farm use (milking); barrels; casks for wine and spirits; and wooden *botijos*. Throughout Galicia, rural carpenters make the sculpted yokes for oxen, with the form varying from area to area, but similar to those made in León, Asturias, and the Basque Country-Navarre region, although the latter have more carved decoration.

222 *Barrel-making is a craft still practiced, especially for keeping vintage wines. An Andalusian bodega*

223 *Galicia, a region of sylvan wealth, has great resources of wood; here, a container for transporting water*

224

224   *Wooden crupper with carved designs.*
Pyrenees of Huesca

225   *Finely sculpted yokes in the market of*
Noya, Pontevedra

226   *Wooden washtubs. Galicia*

225

228

229

227   *Wooden shoes with carved decoration over waterproof layer. Betanzos, La Corunna*

228   *Detail of the hollowing out of a wooden shoe*

229   *Interior of a shop which makes wooden shoes, with the blocks of wood waiting to be planed. Asturias*

A curious article found only in the Pyrenees in the provinces of Lérida and Huesca is a sort of wooden crupper which, like its leather or sailcloth counterpart, serves to keep the pack-saddle from shifting toward the animal's neck. It is made of nettle wood and, once curved, is colored black with a special soot or with pitch.

Then it is carved with a very fine chisel, leaving a white design. The designs are highly decorative geometric motifs made up of squares, latticework, rosettes, spoked wheels, crosses, hearts, and stylized plant designs, which completely cover the surface of the crupper.

Wooden shoes

This type of footwear, very common in the rural areas of cold, rainy, northern Spain, and in all of France, seems to have been used by the Celtic tribes; its widespread use in Catalonia, the Basque Country, Navarre, Asturias, Galicia, and León developed through contact with neighboring France.

These shoes are made by starting with a block of wood which is hollowed out with an appropriate instrument. A

161

light wood such as birch or beech is used, so it is both hard and easy to carve. Because of their function and the material itself, there are few variations in form in spite of the wide geographic distribution; the variations consist of a more or less pointed toe and the presence of a heel or three pegs to lighten the weight of the shoe. In spite of this, we note that the clogs of the Catalonian Pyrenees region are cruder and more archaic in form, with no heel or design, unlike the ones made in **Ripoll** (Barcelona) and **Olot** (Gerona) which are given heels and carved designs and then painted to make them more water-resistant.

Clogs are also used in the Baztán area of Navarre, made of chestnut wood and painted black.

The wooden shoes typically worn by women in the Asturian and Galician villages have three pegs for support, and are made with greater care. This, together with the more graceful

230

230   *A curious scene featuring wooden shoes. Luarca, Santander*

231   *Various types of incised decoration*

232   *Simple, beautiful wooden shoes in a Galician market*

231

162

appearance of being elevated on three pegs and colorfully painted, makes them an attractive, almost refined shoe. They are made in several towns in Asturias—**Grado**, **Puerto de Tarna**, **Luarca**, **Vegadeo**—and in Galicia—**Mos**, **Betanzos**, **Villalba**. They are sold in markets and in shops specializing in such footwear. The decorative carving is done after the shoes are painted, so the designs are white and contrast with the painted color. Usually only the instep is decorated, with geometric, lattice-like, and diamond designs, although they used to be completely decorated in a style similar to the pastoral designs, with zig-zags and floral stylizations in relief.
This footwear, so practical in damp climates, has given way to rubber boots, because the villagers themselves see the wooden shoe (as with so many almost irreplaceable objects of traditional use) as a sign of backwardness and poverty. We have seen some men's wooden shoes which imitated the form of a leather shoe, with the "seams" carved in the wood.

Rural carpenters
In many towns there are unpretentious carpenters, survivors of the long artisan tradition that produced the beautiful balconies, doors, eaves, windows, wardrobes, chests, tables, chairs, and benches, which constitute Spanish folk carpentry. Many of these carpenters now work in phases of building construction, others still make simple, traditional furniture for household use: shelves and brackets, spoon-racks, benches, chairs and tables, or utensils for washing clothes, but they usually work only on order as there is not enough demand to risk accumulating stock.
The furniture which has come to be called rural Andalusian, Majorcan, or Catalonian, polychromed with varying degrees of success, is not bought by

233

any rural Andalusian, Majorcan, or Catalan. It is made in carpenter shops in the cities, specializing in cabinet-making or refined furniture, and has an urban market.
Furniture of light-colored wood, simple and essentially utilitarian, such as *mesas camillas,* round tables covered with round cloths reaching to the floor; kitchen tables; chairs with seat and back of woven rushes; dish-drainers; ironing boards, etc., are all made wherever lathe work is done, essentially in Valencia, Alicante, and Barcelona. They have a wide market, along with other lathed products.

233   Painted decoration on a typical chair in Andalusia

glass

For many centuries, glass was considered a precious luxury material. In the Book of Job (28:17) it is included with gold and precious stones. In the Greco-Roman period, the technique of blowing glass, possibly originating in Syria, was introduced, and glass became a more commonly used material, though still very limited; glass articles were exported from Rhodes and Alexandria to the whole Roman world as luxury items. Work in glass as a luxury material continued until this century, undergoing various technical improvements and changes in style. But our purpose here is to discover still existing production on a popular, unpretentious level, either in blown or molded glass.

Popular production of blown glass for domestic use is very limited and consists of oil and vinegar cruets and *porrones,* the cone-shaped wine bottles with the narrow spout for drinking, which come in two shapes: with a straight neck or a slightly curved neck. They are made in **Palma de Majorca**, **Barcelona**, and **Ollería** (Valencia) and preserve the purity of the traditional forms.

Parallel to this utilitarian production, we find that in both Barcelona and Palma de Majorca, they still make the vessels used in centuries past, with the open work typical of Spanish glassware, but modifying the forms a bit according to changing tastes. The glass of Majorca is an intense green, while that of Barcelona is clear.

The glass kiln of the Pueblo Español in Barcelona has started making reproductions of antique pieces and sells three series of blown glass: the popular series modeled on antique pieces from **Cervelló** and **Mataró** (Barcelona), **Vombodí** (Tarragona), and **Almatret** (Lérida); the series of openwork pieces, of less pure design; and the latticework pieces, adding white strands

234

of glass to the body, reproducing the refined production of the eighteenth century. Here one can see the magical process of glass-blowing, as the shop is open to the public. The glass in its liquid state is like a fiery paste of great plasticity. Now all the kilns use fueloil, as it is cheaper than wood and provides more heat, so that the pieces have fewer imperfections. The imperfections we find in the old articles of popular manufacture, and which give them a characteristic texture, are due to the low temperatures of the traditional kilns, which often did not reach the 1300 °C. needed.

234   *Oil cruet showing traditional form*

235   *Blown glass* botijo *of airy lines, and botlle with the openwork fashionable in the early twentieth century*

236

237

236   Old piece with net decoration

*237   A porrón of elegant lines with
open-work decoration*

*238   Two beautiful old pieces of blown glass
from Catalonia with animal motifs*

With a compact ball of viscous
substance on the end of a long metal
tube, the artisan blows into the tube,
giving shape to a soft, growing form as
if it were a soap bubble. The glass
hardens quickly, but permits the able
artisan to give it the shape desired by
modeling the outside with wooden or
iron tools. With long tongs or scissors
he separates the form from the tube
and continues with the laborious
process of adding new forms if the
piece has various parts. For example,
the spout of the *porrón* must be fused
to the body, and a knob of liquid glass
on the neck of a cruet is stretched to

become the handle which is attached to
the body.

The technique of decorating with open
work is done with the same procedure,
curling a thin tube of glassy paste with
tongs.

Until a very few years ago, beautiful
examples of glass articles for popular
use were made: glasses and bottles,
flasks and pitchers in **Campanet**
(Majorca); and in **Vimbodí,** carafes,
porrones in various shapes, sold in
neighboring areas, cruets, very large
porrones for working in the fields, and
two pieces for ceremonial use: the
"almorratxa", a receptacle with several

240

spouts, used to pour wine in village fiestas, and the little glass *botijos* used by the priest for ceremonial washing at baptisms.

But all these small artisan industries of limited production tend to disappear, victims of financial difficulties and of the new modes of production and consumption.

Molded glass

In the mid-nineteenth century a new industry appeared alongside the making of blown glass, which makes, almost exclusively, household articles: this is the bottle industry. Alcoholic beverages and medicines began to be made commercially, and specific containers were needed for each product. Thus bottle-making establishments appeared, sometimes as extensions of glass-blowing shops, making glass with molds. The popularization of the bottle that contains the product continues today, the product practically identified by the shape of the bottle, as in the cases of anisette, Calisay, and Curaçao, all popular in Spain. Each liquor manufacturer had his models and, after making a plaster mold, hundreds of identical bottles with the client's name reached the market. Clear glass was used for this production, while for pharmaceutical and cosmetic products, turquoise blue, dark green, and topaz were used.

Now automatic production has eliminated the making of new molds and the products are differentiated by the labels, thus facilitating storage and distribution, as well as keeping the cost down.

Many widely consumed beverages still use their nineteenth-century bottles, which have come to be traditional and are invariably present in small-town taverns and fashionable big-city bars alike.

Another aspect of molded glass worth mentioning is the making of glasses

239   *Glowing glass is cut before being applied to piece*

240   *Curious nineteenth-century poster. Display of molded glass bottles. Barcelona*

171

and goblets characteristic of a given beverage or region. Such is the long-stemmed wine glass, called *"cata-vinos"*, used in all of Andalusia for fragrant wines; the thick-sided, shallow glass with a solid base used in northern Spain for drinking *Chacolí,* the wine of the region; the glass of modern lines, called "Bilbao", which is used for drinking *horchata,* a drink usually made from groundnuts; and even the large glass with very thin sides used in Asturias to serve Asturian cider; or the rough glass with concave facets, popularly used in Madrid. There is a geographic distribution of some designs and each of them has a specific use. The same occurs with wine bottles and water bottles for use in bars and restaurants.

There are several toys made of pressed glass of little purity: little boxes in the shape of chickens; miniature candelabra, sugar bowls, and fruit trays; little glasses and salt-cellars. The molds are old and had fallen into disuse but they have come back into style and are being made again, especially in the Levantine region, destined now for a sophisticated domestic market or for export.

241

241, 242   Various glasses used for different wines or in different geographic areas

242

toys

243

Toys of popular tradition

This is the time, perhaps, to take a small inventory of the traditional toys and games all Spaniards have known, used "everywhere" and since "forever" and which no longer form part of the cultural world of Spanish children, since toys have become just another object mass-produced by large industries, a homogenized product subject to the rules of busines competition.

The toys to which we wish to refer are created by the hands of unsophisticated artisans or by small family artisan industries, with rudimentary tools and humble materials: wood, cardboard, paper, lead, etc.

These objects are full of spontaneity and ingenuity, with a special breath of creative ingenuousness linked to the environment in which they are created; they appear before us as true representatives of the spirit of the people. The toys still being made today speak of ways of life almost lost: miniature ceramics, called *"fireta"* or *"escuraeta",* reproduce forms of receptables and kitchen equipment now in disuse in the "grown-up" world: coal-burning stoves, chocolate pots, spoon-holders.

243   *Lovely, ingenuous merry-go-round*

244   *Peddler of simple whistles. Madrid*

174

244

245

246

We shall separate toys into two groups: those of "fantasy" and those which reproduce objects and attitudes of the adult world.

Toys of "fantasy"
Among the most elementary are the noise-making toys: whistles, some as interesting as the *"siurells"* of Majorca, of ancient origin, which for their simplicity and plastic beauty are interesting pieces. They are modeled by hand in clay, like direct sculptures— they surprisingly evoke early Iberian votive offerings— baked, bathed in whitewash and painted with brush strokes in primary colors. The pipe enclosed in the figure is also of clay. These pipes represent human characters, animals, or customs of the rural areas of Majorca, although sometimes they render tribute to the modern world, taking the forms of automobile drivers and tennis players. They are made throughout the year

(in **Sa Cabaneta, Portol,** and **Inca**), mostly by women and children (Madona Bet and Madona Antonia) but they are sold chiefly in the festival of San Marçal (June 30, in Marratxí). This is one of the few pieces of folk art that has survived the massive demands of domestic and foreign tourism; although some forms have degenerated or have undergone "enrichment" (they are glazed, or made in absurd sizes and over-decorated), in general they are still robust, fresh pieces.
Similar to these *"siurells"* or *"xiulets"* are the whistles of **Andújar**, in the form of a rider, gallantly astride a horse or a little bull with a sun between the horns. They are made with the same technique as the rest of the local pottery, painted with blue brush strokes and then glazed. Others, more popular and sold at fairs and festivals, are also made of clay, but painted after glazing with plastic paint. Also in Andújar, there is

a whistle sold only in *romerías* (traditional pilgrimages to local shrines); it is a simple stylization of a dove, in baked clay, as tiny as can be. In **Palma del Río,** they make clay whistles or pipes called "canaries", as they are filled with water and when blown into, make a noise like the warbling of a bird. Other toy whistles, sold in rural fairs and markets, are those made in **Manises,** made with molds and glazed. The lines are jumbled and discarded glaze is used; the result is not artistically very beautiful. Wooden whistles and rattles are made in **Valencia** and **Murcia,** which has an important tradition of toy-making. These are simple pieces of wood, roughly turned and dyed with anilines. Curiously, one of the most used dyes is purple.
A popular figure among nineteenth-century toys, the cardboard and wooden drummer, gave birth to another popular character called

247

248

"Don Nicanor", now made only by a modest Madrid artisan who sells his toys in Madrid's Sunday flea market, the Rastro; there, both "Don Nicanor" and his creator have achieved popularity. This artisan, Señor Duque, made another toy until a few years ago, which was a little human or animal figure which appeared inside a cardboard tube and had a whistle worked by the up-and-down movement of the little puppet; he called them "Curritos" and a particularly beautiful one was a bull with a defiant pair of lead horns; the other characters were mostly bullfighters or dignified gentlemen with long mustaches.

As these simple, elementary toys are made in small quantity and cannot be commercialized, they are found only near very popular commercial forms and almost always sold directly by their creators. Such is the case with Señor Antonio, who sells his special figures in the bargain market Los

Encantes, in Barcelona. They are not whistles, but some have movable parts, such as the tambourine player. He uses industrial materials and the designs are somewhere between surrealistic and popular; the names he gives to his characters are truly poetic.

Another object used in play is the cricket cage. Children hunt and capture crickets and put them in little wood-and-wire cages bought in markets and at fairs. They feed them and take care of them so that the crickets will sing and entertain them. In **Villafranca de los Caballeros**, they make cricket cages of baked clay, with a tiny door and many small holes, but with these cages, the child can only hear the cricket because this cage is opaque and almost solid, unlike the cages of reed or wire.

Other imaginative toys are those we might define as "creators of rhythm in space", and which are a mixture of the user's coordination and a challenge to (or taking advantage of) the laws of

245, 246   Clay whistles showing interesting iconography. Majorca

247, 248   Painted clay whistles on bullfighter theme, typical of Andújar, Jaén

177

249

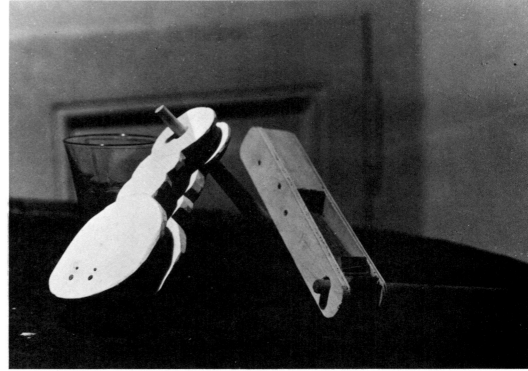

250

249 *Ingenuous wooden bird which moves down a wire, pecking in imitation of a woodpecker*

250 *Wooden rattles,* carracas, *made by a shepherd*

251 *Detail of one of the merry-go-round horses. Granada*

178

gravity. In this group we find teetotums and whipping tops, which, with small variations, are made everywhere wood is worked on a lathe. Until a few years ago there was a wide variety of colors, sizes, quality of the wood, and design; now there is less, and it won't be long before these toys disappear altogether. The same is true of pinwheels and kites. There is a plastic version of pinwheels, in bright colors, which has some of the charm of the pinwheels made of colored paper. There is also an oriental version of the brightly colored kites made of reed and onionskin paper; this version is made of cloth in complex shapes and hasn't the colorful tail of the traditional kites. One can still find kites in toy shops and basket shops, but the tradition of going out to the country to fly kites has been lost, and soon kites will not be sold at all. Another toy seldom made today is the "tightrope walker", which spins around a cord attached to two sticks which are moved in and out. It is usually made of pressed wood and painted with anilines. Another toy of this type is the "woodpecker", which moves rhythmically along a wire by means of a simple mechanism; or the little chicks that peck away at the center of a small board thanks to a weight which is swung slowly; or the cymbal player, a rough figure which, when a spring is pressed, clangs two tin cymbals together. These are all made in small family workshops in homes, along with other daily occupations.

Toys that reproduce objects and attitudes of the adult world
This is a wide field, and we shall mention only some of the toys still being made today which offer a wider variety of production.
The sets of kitchenware for little girls (now often made industrially, of tin) have different, charming names in

253

they stick together and must be pulled apart.

In **Manises,** an important pottery center, they make a great variety of small pieces of this type, of white earthenware with floral designs, which are sent to toy shops everywhere. Another aspect of this adult world scaled down to child size is wooden furniture. In **Valencia,** they make sofas, chairs, *mesas camillas,* and rocking chairs of light-colored wood and rushes.

In **Lanjarón** (Granada), they make delicate furniture of fine wicker, reminiscent of the style of furniture made popular by Levantines returned from the New World: candle tables, high-backed armchairs, sofas, and chairs.

There are probably no more of the family workshops that made the lovely cardboard dolls called "Pepas" or "Peponas", that used to be sold at fairs and, with their flat shoes and poor dress, were like coarse copies of real little girls and boys. But so many of these dolls were made that they can still be found in some old shops and stores. They were made almost exclusively in Catalonia and Valencia (in the city of Valencia, the tradition of working in papier mâché and cardboard still thrives, thanks to the annual Fallas) although there were small local shops in many cities and rural areas.

These dolls could be rigid except for movable arms, or they might have a cloth or cardboard body with movable legs—they could sit—and the arms made by sections and attached later with the seam hidden by abundant, rough paint. The appearance of these dolls is reflected in common expressions: "You look like a *pepona",* or, "You look like a ten-cent *pepa"*—because a maker of these dolls in Barcelona sold them for ten *céntimos*—meaning someone looks ungainly, strange, or not physically attractive.

252   Figures of folk iconography with touches of ingenuous surrealism. Barcelona

253   Toys that are miniature reproductions of the adult world. Little wooden table and miniature crockery from Arjonilla, Jaén

On pages 182 and 183:

254   Wooden chairs

255   Horse of molded cardboard. Santa María de Barberá, Barcelona

256   Ingenuous cardboard horses

different areas: *"escuareta"* in the **Vall D'Uxó** (Castellón), *"fireta"* in **La Bisbal** (Gerona), *"miniaturas"* and *"lillos"* in **Arjonilla** (Jaén), *"ajuaritos"* in **Sorbas** (Almería). They are all miniature reproductions of kitchenware used by adults, made in glazed or unglazed clay.

Surprisingly, sometimes these sets include pieces no longer used at all in family kitchens. Other sets, such as the ones made in Sorbas, are made as gifts; all the pieces come inside a pan and, although the pieces are separate, the potter pours a few drops of glaze over them when he puts them in the kiln, so

181

These cardboard dolls disappeared with the arrival of celluloid dolls made in Germany.

The making of cardboard horses and bulls, in **Sabadell** and **Barcelona** has fared better. They are still made with the same patterns, but they are not so carefully finished and painted as some years ago.

It is difficult to find these kinds of toys in toy shops; one has to go to rural markets and especially to the markets set up in big cities before Three Kings Day (January 6).

Lead toys.

This old tradition, most likely imported from Italy, as the first little figures were made by an Italian, were popular until the early twentieth century. When it became known that lead is poisonous, the market for them decreased considerably.

The procedure consists of pouring molten lead, or tin mixed with antimony, into a two-part mold of slate. The thick liquid goes through a vertical opening between the two plates to fill in the mold. When it is cooled, the mold is opened and the extraneous material around the edges is trimmed off. Then the molded figures (soldiers, little chapels, flower vases, fans, sail boats, trains) are painted.

So popular were these toys that they were sold not by the piece, but by weight.

Figures for Nativity scenes, especially small animals, were also cast in metal, but this was done in family workshops. At present, one can find evidence of this production in the fairs or markets where Nativity scene figures are sold; and in Madrid, Juan Fernández still makes little lead soldiers.

The children's games that consisted of battles of lead soldiers are still played, but the soldiers are plastic, and there is a wider variety of figures.

254

255

elements of popular theater

257

Puppets and marionettes

By puppets or marionettes, we mean small, articulated figures representing persons or animals, moved by means of threads, springs, or simply with the hand. Covarrubias, in 1611, in his work, *Tesoro de la Lengua Castellana,* first mentions puppets (in Spanish, *títeres,* which, according to the Royal Academy, is an onomatopoetic word), describing them as little figures which foreign persons display in a little stage, concealing themselves behind a wooden castle, and causing the figures to move while emitting special sounds, as if they themselves were the puppets.

The history of puppets is ancient, and they appear, in one form or another, in all the classical cultures. It seems that during the Middle Ages, puppet shows were essentially religious and later took on the themes of popular legends or popularized legends of literary origin; the public was made up mostly of common folk and the contact with this public finally produced the humorous or comical puppet show.

These comical characters achieved the greatest popular acceptance, so much so that the names of the central characters, Christofi Polichinello and

Monsieur Guignol (who were always the same) provide the popular names for the genre: *polichinelas, "pulchinells", "putxinellis",* and *"guignol".*

In small towns, puppet theater was performed periodically by traveling artists. The hand puppet, with wooden head and hands and a hollow body of cloth into which the puppeteer slipped his hand to make the puppet move, began to be used. This theatrical genre, schematic and simple, came more and more to be directed toward children. The evolution of the Italian Pulcinella produced the following types and

258

in imitation of the professionals' wooden puppets.

It is a form of play still popular in Catalonia, where fondness for puppets persisted long enough to coincide with the return to popularity of puppets all over the world. Thus, one can still find cardboard puppets and puppet theaters in small-town toy shops, made in artisan workshops of ten or fifteen years ago. Sometimes the same artisans also made clay figures for Nativity scenes.

The toy industry, recovering from the "plastic fever", has gone back to using cardboard and traditional archetypes, but the painting and finishing have lost the ingenuous rusticity of years past.

Giants and "cabezudos"

These are monstrous figures of medieval origin which, with their presence, magnify the processions of Corpus Christi Day.

Their great heads, torsos, arms, and hands are made of cardboard and from the waist down they are made of a frame of basketry or light wood. They are two or three times taller than a person, and they move in a sacerdotal fashion over the tiny feet of the man inside.

The tradition is common to all Levantine towns and there are pronounced differences in their symbolisms. The giants are warriors, knights, kings, or, as in Majorca, peasants. They appear always in pairs, a man and a woman. The woman is dressed like a medieval lady or queen, although in Valencia and Barcelona in the nineteenth century she provided a preview of the next year's fashions. Usually, they are the property of the parish or the town's governing body, which must take care of them, keeping them in good condition, dressing them, and taking them out for processions. Many towns have both Moors and Christians among their giant couples,

257   Cardboard puppets of popular characters

258   Puppets of the well-known puppeteer Didó, in polychromed wood, preserved in the Museo del Teatro in Barcelona

259   Traditional giants. Barcelona

260   Carnival masks of molded cardboard

traditions: Don Cristóbal, in Castile; Cristófal and Tófol, in Catalonia; Tirisitis, in Alicante; Teresetes, in the Balearic Islands; Tia Norica (marionette technique) in Andalusia; and Barriga Verde in Galicia. The puppeteers were the creators of the puppets and the scripts, and both were family property. The puppets used well into the twentieth century were carved in wood, and the standard popular characters were: the protagonist, his female companion, his rival, a know-it-all old crone, the devil, and Death. The amateur and children's version was done in cardboard, molded and painted

187

which forces the youngsters to express their preferences.

The giants' retinue is formed by young volunteers wearing inmmense cardboard heads. They are called *cabezudos* ("having a large head") and symbolize the common folk. Their expressions are caricaturesque and crude and they perform an intentionally grotesque pantomime around the giants. Sometimes, as in Tortosa, they represent the various social classes, with a clear distinction between fine gentlemen and peasants. These pieces of molded cardboard are made on order by specialized shops in Valencia and Barcelona. But orders are infrequent.

Some festivals have, besides these characters, cardboard monsters, fearsome and exotic creatures, like Romanesque representations of terrible incarnations of evil. In Catalonia there are two very popular ones: the Cucafera, of Tortosa, and the Guita of the Patum festival in Berga.

The parades of giants, *cabezudos,* and local monsters are becoming rarer and rarer, although they form part of the "typical" elements preserved at all costs for the sake of pretentious and stale tourist appeal.

These old religious-pagan customs had some meaning in a certain cultural milieu; as an unequaled spectacle, they are now relics forced to play a mediocre role as tourist attraction.

261   Two impressive male giants dancing in the Corpus Christi festival in Berga, Barcelona

262   Recently made giants inspired by traces of Roman iconography. Castelltersol, Barcelona

263   Grotesque cabezudos, *exaggeratedly realistic. Santiago de Compostela, La Corunna*

262

191

votive offerings

264

Votive offerings

These simple garments and ornaments can still be found in churches and chapels in the cities and in innumerable rural hermitages. It is a world of magic and tenderness, which clothes the images of the most generous saints. Sometimes the objects offered are very personal: a bride's veil, or her braids, a little boy's suit, a cripple's crutches, or even the keys and steering wheels of automobiles, now that fatal disease has a rival.

Along with these, there are offerings we can consider folk art, for their simplicity or for the shapes they take, the paintings on wood or glass, relating the perils the giver has experienced, the offerings in silver plate and those in wax.

Paintings on wood or glass

These are small scenes without frame or glass covering, showing, in the top of the scene, the saint or saints invoked in making the vow, and often they include a brief text giving names, date, and the miracle bestowed. The paintings are childish and rough, but are a source of information about the interiors of homes, furniture, apparel, tools, and the simple legends in which rural and city dwellers believe.

264   Votive offerings on wood and reliquaries, property of the Museo Etnológico del Pueblo Español, Hispanic Section

265   Nineteenth-century votive offerings on wood

These representations of miracles were made by professional "saint painters" who also made images of saints.

In the beautiful collection in the Museo de Artes e Industrias Populares in Barcelona (or the Hispanic Section of the Museo Etnológico) there are votive offerings dated from the seventeenth century to the early twentieth century, and most of them are done on wood. These offerings are no longer made; the shortage of "saint painters" and the advent of photography have put an end to this form of showing gratitude, and it has been replaced with other, cruder forms, such as the steering wheel mentioned above.

Nevertheless, this simple way of relating events is still valued, and has its followers and collectors. In **Mataró** (Barcelona), a Catalan industrialist paints votive offerings in his spare time (an avocational "saint painter"), in which he relates family occurrences and anecdotes. But surely no one who needs a votive offering knows of him, and this form of religious thank-offering has been abandoned.

In **Madrid,** a young lady from Extremadura, named Susana, used to sell antiques, votive offerings, and Divine Shepherdesses painted on glass, from Extremadura and Andalusia, in the Rastro on Sundays. One day she began to include, among the nineteenth-century painted glass, others she had done herself; it was getting more and more difficult to find these examples of popular devotion. She now exhibits her work. She works on glass, painting on the back and using gold leaf to enrich the effect. She takes her inspiration from old models but always adds her own elementary decorative touch and her own version of the anecdote.

Votive offerings in silver plate
These are factory-made, with a die, or cut by hand in sheets of silver. The

266

266 *Decorative design in the style of traditional painted glass. Madrid*

267 *Ingenuous composition on glass. Madrid*

267

268

269

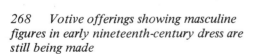

268   Votive offerings showing masculine figures in early nineteenth-century dress are still being made

269   Metal votive offerings are being made now with traditional molds

270   Technique of painting glass on reverse side

molds were most likely made by silversmith apprentices, as the forms are simple and unsophisticated. Sanctuaries in Andalusia, Catalonia, and Majorca are full of these little flat statues, 7 to 20 centimeters high. They usually have a little silk string by which they are hung near the image of the saint to which they are dedicated. They are charming figures of men or women, or of separate parts of the body: arms, hands, eyes, breasts, male heads, frontal or in profile; or figures of animals, especially un Majorca: horses, pigs, donkeys; or ships.

It is most unlikely that they are still being made, but they can still be found in jewelry shops near churches. The patterns are from the early nineteenth century, particularly noticeable in the arms of women, which are adorned in the imitation-French style of the times. The human figures are of a popular sort, detailing wearing apparel, and of course, it is harder to determine the dates of eyes, breasts, and hands. They were made in silversmith shops in Barcelona, Majorca, Jaén, and Seville.

Votive offerings in wax and candles
In sanctuaries and wax-chandlers' shops, we can see that persons suffering

272

ailments of head, ears, eyes, arms, hands, legs, feet, heart, and even breasts, in the case of nursing mothers, offer reproductions of these members, cast or molded in wax.

The molds are very simple and the material unappealing for anyone who wishes to find more than the religious content of the figures. We must note, however, the surrealistic sensation these pieces evoke. In Portugal, these very physiological forms are enriched by the presence of houses and animals made of wax.

Candles are also worthy of mention, although in the past few years the atractiveness and decoration of some of them have dwindled. In **Barcelona,** they used to make candles wreathed by flowers; they were offered at baptisms by the godmother, and the flowers were pink or blue, depending on the sex of the child. They haven't been made for ten years, since the death of the artisan who made the bell-shaped flowers. In Madrid, in the typical old street of Atocha, there is a wax-chandler's that sells lovely baptism candles adorned with strips of colors, multicolored flowers, and strips of wax curled with pincers.

271   Flowered baptismal candles

272   Votive offerings in wax in the Cartes Sanctuary, Albacete

201

273

274

273   *Candles with ruffled decoration made with pincers*

274   *Front of a chandler's shop in Madrid*

202

nativity scene figures

275

The Nativity scene

Jesus' birth was represented in
Romanesque capitals and frescoes,
but the truly popular representation of
the Christmas Mystery is attributed to
Saint Francis of Assisi, who celebrated
the midnight mass in a stable,
mystically and poetically recalling the
humble setting where the Nativity
took place.

His initiative was copied in convents
and churches where, based on the
Gospel according to St. Luke and St.
Matthew, the whole mystery of the
Nativity was acted out by real people.
The Nativity scene figures, both those
made by artists of religious imagery and
those made by popular artisans, are
modeled on those who acted out the
Christmas story, first in convents and
then in parish churches. And so the
custom reached the homes of the
people in the form of the Nativity
scene, in Spanish called simply *belén*
(Bethlehem).

Chronicles from the eighteenth century
speak of elaborate Nativity scenes set
up in convents, churches, the houses of
nobles, and public places, but they do
not mention the homemade figures
used by a lower-class public, most
probably inspired by those made by
Italian and Spanish artists of religious
imagery. The technique is unrefined
and the dress either traditional or
modeled with varying accuracy on
Biblical times. But we believe that this
popular industry already existed
because we find in a description of the
Festival of Santa Llùcia in Barcelona,
in 1786: "many little houses for
Nativity scenes, little goats, Herod's
palaces, lovely figures in clay and
pasteboard, images of saints and
shepherds, oxen, mules, and other
animals". The chronicle does not
explain the characteristics of these
figures, but we can suppose that,

276

277

275   *Nativity scene figures, showing ingenuous Biblical representations in the angelic style of the turn of the century, made in the workshops of Murcia*

276   *Little house for use in Nativity scene, made of cork with plant elements simulating trees*

277   *Charming bucolic scene, traditionally part of the Nativity scene in Majorca*

although most of the figures were of "cultured" origin, if the festival was large and well-attended, there must have been little figures for persons of modest means.

In today's fairs where Nativity scene figures are sold, and in shops which sell these figures during the Christmas season, we find the classic clay figures competing with plastic ones, little houses of cork and cardboard, plants made of moss and wood, bridges and villages, churches and barns. The clay figures sold in the peninsula are almost all made in the two most active and enterprising centers: **Murcia** and

Barcelona. The Majorca figures are sold only locally and to not appear in the large markets mentioned above. Rather, all the architecture which forms the structure of the Nativity scene is locally made by artisans in each town. In Madrid, for example, the least expensive figures are from Murcia, and those considered elegant, from Olot and Barcelona, but the rest of the components come from small family industries in and around Madrid.

Murcian figures

There is a large production of clay figures, which are sold in a wide area; we could almost say they have inundated the market.

They are made in **Murcia** (the town of Lorca, which used to make them, hardly makes them now, as the demand has been absorbed by shops in the provincial capital) in two types of workshops and two types of figures. The elaborate baroque figures made from late nineteenth-century molds and modeled on the works of famous sculptors or artists of religious iconography (such as that of Salcillo, of 1780, made for the noble house of Riquelme) are made in large shops. This type of figure responds to

278

279

280

a "museum" concept—the showcase manger scene—and has been in fashion for more than forty years among the well-to-do, who perhaps also bought popular figures for their children to play with. This taste for the baroque style has been changed by the desire to be "modern", which translates into changes in the designs of the figures, reducing them to curios, stereotyped by false stylizations.

A completely different line is that of the simple, elementary figures, made with elementary molds. They are made in small family shops in the family's spare time, dividing the chores among family members. It is these we wish to describe, as each of the places they are made produces typical characters which distinguish them from the figures made in Majorca or Barcelona.

The jovial muleteers, a man and a woman, transporting goods on the back of a mule; the women with kerchiefs on their heads, carrying baskets of musk-

melon and watermelon; the "anunciata" made up of shepherds in sheepskin dress, gathered around a cooking pot (surely containing rice or *gachas,* a pap common in the area), listening to an angel who is hanging from a tree bare of leaves; the shepherdesses, wearing hats with the brim turned up in front, gracefully carrying their offerings... All these popular and rural prototypes appear among groups of figures "Biblically" dressed, representing market scenes, such as a butcher's shop with skinned animal carcasses and purple-painted scales; or domestic chores, such as a woman setting bread in an oven, another doing wash, another filling jugs with water. And last, a complete scene showing concrete events in the infancy of Jesus: knocking at the door of the inn and Joseph's carpenter's shop.

The figures are painted after baking with bright, lively colors. The finishing

is no longer done so carefully, as these pieces must compete with plastic figures, and there are very few families who still make them.

The Majorcan figures

On the island of Majorca, there is a very limited production of handmade Nativity scene figures, and they are almost unknown outside the islands. Some years ago, they were made in the potteries of Manacor, Inca, and in the capital itself. Now the only two artisan families that make them live in Palma. In one of the families, the only person who does this work is an elderly woman, *doña* Francisca Fuster, who makes only shepherds. The other family makes the traditional groups of village folk performing their chores, which will form the town of the Nativity scene in which the "mysteries"— Biblical passages—are of "cultured" origin, and come from Murcia.

281

282

This whole popular world which surrounds the religious figures is a faithful representation of the rural life in the islands, with its characteristic intimacy and seclusion. Some of the groups, delicately painted in bright tones and robust colors, reproduce the interior of a Majorcan kitchen. Others show a peasant girl watering flowers or hanging wash to dry. Others show a wheel for drawing water and the mule that moves it, or a man by a barn, or a farmer plowing a minutely detailed field. All the individual figures, shepherds going to the stable, are carrying gifts characteristic of the islands: typical pastries, sausages, and cheeses. There is also a series of musicians with pipes, flutes, drums, timbrels, and *zambombas,* a sort of drum consisting of a jar tightly covered with a skin, through which a reed is moved up and down.

Among the figures of animals, a beautiful black and red turkey deserves special mention. Its tail is open and the legs and feet are simply two wires stuck in a green base. It is made in all sizes and is called an *"indiot"*. It is of extraordinary simplicity.

In the places where thay make the whistles called *"siurells",* they have started making Nativity scenes with the *siurells* themselves. The best results are to be found in **Sa Cabaneta,** where Madó Bet makes a small cave with the central figures, decorated only with a border of cockle-shells, and another Nativity scene with separate figures in which the traditional forms of the farmer or man on horseback are transformed into the shepherds or the Three Kings. The other essential elements are done very simply.

The Nativity scene in Catalonia
It is surely in Catalonia where the tradition of the Nativity scene, here called *"pesebre"* (manger) has had its deepest roots in folk tradition and has

278   The muleteer, a popular Murcian figure

279   Realistic, ingenuous scene of the sacrifice of the paschal lamb in the Murcian Nativity scene

280   Group of shepherds in a simple Annunciation

281   Delicate Majorcan figures wearing traditional dress and carrying products characteristic of the island

282   Nativity scene figure made with the technique of the "siurells", a recent innovation

been most widely practiced. There have been exhaustive studies by scholars of folklore and interest by all types of collectors.

In the nineteenth century, along with the creative work of master sculptors who worked with this type of figures, there were six artisan centers where Nativity scene figures were made. These were: **Olot**, so identified with the making of religious images that it is called "the city of the saints"; **Manresa**; **Mataró**; **Selva del Camp**; **Tortosa**; and the city of **Barcelona**. These centers influenced the surrounding areas, and the result is a strong and constant presence of the Nativity scene in the Christmas festivities.

At present, this production is centered in Barcelona, from where it is sent to all areas of Catalonia and even other markets farther away. Production has become thus concentrated because the limited markets used to be supplied by two or three artisans and, once these disappeared, there wasn't enough demand to perpetuate the tradition, and the orders went to the area with the greatest concentration of artisan workshops.

We shall not go into the production of the artisans making figures of artistic creation, but rather in that of those artisans who work with simple traditional molds, created by their families, and which tend to represent the special world of the Catalonian cities and rural areas.

The panorama is wide: from the detailed miniatures (some as small as 3 to 10 cm.) made by a diminutive artisan, Roser Cotanda, to the curious and interesting plants and flowers made by the Bertrán family, to the figures in nineteenth-century Barcelona style, made by the Vidal family.

In the festival of Santa Llùcia, across from the Cathedral of Barcelona, the array of little stalls attests to the

283

constancy of these artisans, if not to their financial prosperity. Most of them are from families with a tradition in making Nativity scenes; the prices are low—today they would be called "competitive"—and really do not cover the hours of work and dedication required.

But we shall value them only when they are gone, though this will be in the not-distant future.

It is curious that the traditional market expects prices that are not profitable to the artisan, as if the world of production had not changed. Every figure requires so much handling!

283   Tender reproduction in the Nativity scene of rural Majorcan scenes, now nearly nonexistent

284   Carefully made figures showing a museum-inspired concept of the Nativity scene

285   A miniature reproduction in cork of a mountain village

286   Two figures of the village priest, from traditional molds

287   The inevitable fisherman, in typical Catalonian dress

288   There can be no Christmas scene without miniature domestic animals

290

289   Two typical characters in Catalonian Nativity scenes

290   Small Catalonian farmhouse and the rural elements that surround it: barn, cart, and well

Molding, drying, painting with several colors, giving each figure its distinguishing attributes, storing, transporting, selling—and for a price of ten or twenty *pesetas.*

Figures in the popular tradition, representing rural types, wear the traditional headgear of Catalonia: men, a sort of Phrygian hat, and women a net over their hair. In Catalonia, the figures, while popular, do not portray traditional customs as often as the *santons* of Provence, or the groups of Majorca or Murcia. The rural characters are always separate figures which do not form part of a group: shepherds,

hunters, fishermen with fishing poles, women spinning... We find the *costumbrista* types: the traditional night watchman of the streets of Barcelona, the woman selling chestnuts, the priest under an umbrella, and the classic and scatalogical *"caganer"* (peasant using meadow as "privy"), never absent from the Nativity scene.

To accommodate all these figures, there is a section with little villages made of cork, built on steep mountains; many varieties of Catalonian farm buildings; and newly gathered clumps of moss, covered

291

292

*291   Little figures for sale at the
Christmas fair or market*

*292   A scene from the fair of Santa Llùcia,
with expectant youngsters*

with flour "snow", serving as fields and
meadows.

A genuinely local atmosphere, with
landscape, houses, and villages, is most
carefully portrayed in the construction
of the farm buildings and the rural
elements that surround them: carts,
barns for storing hay, animal pens. An
old artisan, long a maker of Nativity
scene figures, Señor Riera, very ill as
these lines are being written, has made,
at our urging, a collection of different
types of these Catalonian farm
buildings, called *masías.* They are made
of cork and cardboard and painted in
great detail.

Fairs and selling of Nativity scene figures
In Valencia, Palma, Madrid, and
Barcelona, fairs are held where only
figures, plants, and trees for making
Nativity scenes are sold. The fairs begin
between December 8 (Immaculate
Conception) and December 21 (St.
Thomas), depending on the city.
Figures are sold in neighborhood herb
shops and in village crockery shops. It
is difficult to find these figures during
the rest of the year, so the fairs are a
necessary part of the season, as are small
markets where fir trees and other items
more or less related to Christmas are sold.
Except in Madrid, where it became

popular in the nineteenth century, the
Nativity scene is unknown in Castile.
Nor is it popular in Asturias, León, or
Extremadura. In Valencia, Castellón,
and Alicante, there are live
representations of the Nativity,
replacing the Nativity scene of
inanimate figures. In Andalusia, there
is a limited production based in the
potteries of **Triana** (Seville) and **Granada**
clearly reminiscent of the figures from
Murcia. The massive invasion of figures
from Murcia and Olot (Gerona), with an
artistic leaning, satisfies the needs in
those places where the Nativity scene
is an "imported" custom.

214

forms of bread

293

Breads and sweets

An important exhibit titled Cookies and Bread was held in the Museum of Contemporary Crafts in New York, in 1966. There, cookie cutters and breads from many parts of the world and many periods were shown. The contents included everything from fifteenth-century German cracker molds with noble coats-of-arms, to a series of round loaves of archaic simplicity, which have been made since the Roman *panis candius,* with almost no variation. Spain does not have the refined tradition of cake and cookie molds such as we find in the central and northern European countries of Austria, Poland, Hungary, Germany, Switzerland, Holland, and Belgium; nor the tradition of Christmas offerings in the form of delicate sweet cookies—Swiss *tirggel*—made with old, beautifully worked wooden molds. In Spain, the social or religious celebrations are accompanied by the making of special breads and sweets, as a survival of an ancient magical-religious rite which has always considered bread a sacred element; suffice it to remember such common manifestations as the wedding or birthday cake, or the

293   *Traditional, popular Majorcan sweet roll, "ensaimada", with the dough always wound snail-fashion, however large or small*

294   *Breads in a small town's bread shop. La Frontera, Cuenca*

216

Spanish *roscón,* a cake in the shape of a circle used in the celebration of Three Kings Day, not made with a mold, but creating complicated designs with the dough itself, as we find in the San Blas bread, the bread of **Yecla** (Murcia), or the loaves of **Chinchón** (Madrid). The latter have acquired such fame that travelers buy them as decorative pieces, and so they are baked daily.

But the ordinary bread used every day also offers so many local variations in form and design because of the various kinds of flour, the preferences of traditional bakers, and the demands of the consumers, that we believe the study and classification of something so familiar and humble is a worthy undertaking.

This work is arduous, as the material can be preserved only a short time, and molds must be made of each of the loaves so that its shape and characteristics can be preserved. Pérez Contel, an industrious Valencian scholar, has assembled a rich collection. The large Andalusian loaves with a smooth surface which the baker pricks in a regular pattern, "smooth bread", or with only two vertical lines crossed by two horizontal lines, "crust bread"; the Catalonian bread called *"pá de tres crostons",* with a thick, rough crust forming three protuberances at the ends; the large, solid Galician loaves of rye bread; or the loaves of Madrid with a cross in the middle. All make up a whole world of shapes and textures. The homogenization of flours and the use of flours not previously used in bread, the centralization of the bakers' work in large baking industries, and the technically uniform ovens all mean that the diversity we still find today will disappear.

Bread for children

These small loaves, made to be eaten by children, and which include animal

295

296

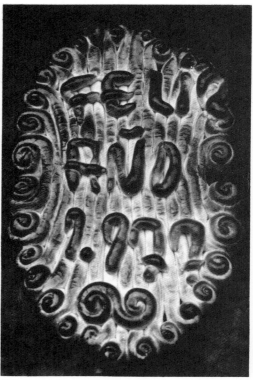

297

218

298

300

299

295   *Holiday sweets*

296, 297   Samples of unusual forms that bread takes in Chinchón, Madrid

298   Selling the great loaves made in small towns

299   Different kinds of bread of varying preparation and qualities. Pastrana, Guadalajara

300   Various shapes of bread with different cuts in crust. Vilafranca del Penedés, Barcelona

219

and other shapes, have their origin in the tradition of making a special loaf the day the family bread was baked in towns and rural villages. In well-off families, a sweet loaf was made for the youngsters; in families of more modest means, the sweet bread was substituted by animal shapes which the mother made of the same dough and baked at the same time as the bread. The shapes, with varying degrees of refinement, represented roosters, little bulls, or human figures, and were adorned and enriched with cumin seed.

This custom persists in some villages where the women still bake bread weekly or fortnightly, but what we wish to note here is how this custom has been transplanted to the cities, where it has flourished, although these little loaves are sold only in the small shops that sell only bread.

Barcelona is the city where we find them most. The bakeries that make them are usually located in heavily populated neighborhoods and this bread is usually made twice a day, early in the morning and in early afternoon, so it is fresh when the children get out of school. This bread is not expensive and is made with regular bread dough. The shapes are simple and without decorative pretentions: swans, giraffes, snails, octopi, camels, pistols, ladders, scissors, and human forms. And, a sign of the times, television personalities, taken from a series popular years ago ("The Saint") and a feline form intended to be "the pink panther" of cartoon fame.

The bakeries that make these surely consider them to be good for business, as they have incorporated a rural custom that was nearly lost, and maintained and expanded it. And here we must appreciate the enduring capacity for play among our children, who would rather eat a snail or a ladder than a piece of bread or a roll.

301

The pilgrimage figures of San Andrés de Teixido

Every year on the eighth of September, a beautiful and unsettling *romería*, or pilgrimage, is celebrated in the village of San Andrés de Teixido, near Cedeira (Lugo). Thousands of pilgrims attend, accompanied by the friend *que non foi de vivo* (who didn't go when he was living).

The pilgrims must return from the *romería* with the branch of San Andrés (St. Andrew), and so they search the area around the hermitage for small branches of yew, a stick of hazlenut wood or, those who want to marry, a

301   A large, wreath-shaped loaf. Alarcón, Cuenca

302   Figure representing San Andrés, made of bread and colored with anilines in San Andrés de Teixido, La Corunna

303   In front of the hermitage, a woman selling sanandreses *during the annual pilgrimage. San Andrés de Teixido, La Corunna*

304   Urban version of the varied animal shapes of special breads that village mothers used to make for their children when they did the fortnightly baking. Barcelona

305

306

"love herb" which carries with it the beneficial virtues of the Saint.

It is the custom to hang *"sanandreses"* from the branches. These are small figures made of unleavened bread, homemade and colored with anilines, which women and children offer for a modest price at the sanctuary, calling them "relics of the Saint".

These little figures have a special charm for their forms and colors. The traditional shapes included only human figures, doves, hands, and braided circles. The other forms that we find today are due to the creative expansion of the mysteries of the Saint by a now deceased member of a family which for many generations had made *"sanandreses"*. The human figures may be of a man or a woman, with arms extended, or in a pious attitude with the hands crossed over the chest. There is a pictorial symbolism in the stances, but it should not be interpreted by the same people who make them. The

doves may have wings spread, or closed, with a knot around them. On the chest there is a ring so they can be hung from the braches. The open hand, with its five fingers, is like a survival of magic rituals. There are three other figures related to the legendary arrival of St. Andrew to these places: the boat, the anchor, and the ladder he used to reach land. There are also figures of fish, wheels, hearts, and clover leaves. And crucifixes and small altars.

Now, almost all the women of the village make *"sanandreses"*, and each creates her own style. They color them with red, yellow, and blue anilines. They used to be painted by dipping each half in a different color; now it is done either by dipping or with a brush, achieving a greater richness of color. This pilgrimage with its *"sanandreses"* is a celebration that will endure, as there are even Galicians who have emigrated to other countries and return in September to join in the *romería*.

305   *Detail of special bread for children*

306   *Three "saints" showing variations in decoration*

paper as ornament

Paper cut-outs; doilies

Cutting out scenes or decorative motifs in paper is a custom common to many countries, although in some—Mexico, Poland, or Portugal—it surpasses the homemade quality found in others. In Spain, there is limited use of paper as decoration but it would be worthwhile to mention some forms which, although they have never acquired the dimensions of a true craft, are popular creations which are soon to be lost.

One of these forms is the paper rosette which has come to replace the lacy wafers used to adorn the traditional Majorcan Nativity scenes. They are hung above the scene and symbolize the weeks of Lent and the days from the beginning of the year until Passion Week. This work is now done only in a few convents and by two persons in Palma.

Another tradition, which probably has its origin in the refined lace-edged or embroidered cloth doilies used to serve small cakes and other sweets, is that of paper doilies imitating complicated lace, which are used in pastry shops. Although they are made by machine—perforating cylinders—they should not be considered of industrial manufacture, as they can only be made within a concept of hand-crafting, in small establishments which tend to die out, as the process includes costly work done by hand.

Likewise deserving of consideration are the border designs or stencils for making repeated designs in rooms and on windowpanes of many rural houses. This type of ornamentation, of folk origin, can still be seen in many places. The border designs can be bought in stores that sell industrial paints, but the small artisan shops where paper doilies as well as the perfect little stencils were made have ceased to be.

The garlands of colored paper and cut-out fringe that used to decorate

307

the streets during festivals are also disappearing, replaced either by strings of electric light bulbs or by nothing at all. The tradition of decorating the streets with colored paper is still kept in **Morella** (Castellón) in the Sexennial Festival. The decorations are made by the residents of each street, working all year long at cutting and gluing colored paper.

Kitchen shelf paper

Today this paper which can be seen adorning the kitchen shelves in city and village alike is entirely mass-produced. But it deserves mention here

307   Cut colored paper forms a delicate, ephemeral ceiling at traditional festivals

308   Shelf paper dresses up kitchen shelves, in hopeful imitation of embroidered cloth

226

310

311

because of its origins, the various ways it was made, and especially because its designs constitute a good sampling of peculiar popular tastes (in one study on the subject, two thousand different designs have been identified).

It began as a humble version of the order and attractiveness of the pantries and kitchens of the wealthy, who used delicate fabrics or lace to adorn the shelves. Its use on a popular level probably began with copies of this fine cloth in paper or in simpler cloth, and acquired its own language and expression by 1870, when printing by means of cylinders became widespread.

From this time on, the presses of Valencia and Barcelona produced a multitude of designs which were sold throughout the country.

That the commercial outlets chosen were those shops frequented mostly by women (groceries, notions shops, and stores which sell household cleaning

articles) clearly indicated that this paper was aimed at a female public And the themes, which reflect general tendencies in graphic arts, are child- and woman-oriented: imitation of lace edging or mosaics (owing to the origins of shelf paper), folkloric themes or pleasant scenes of picnics in the country, strolls, little birds, flowers, butterflies, etc. We should mention that masculine elements seldom appear and when they do, it is always in a very traditional role: a man fishing or hunting.

Before it disappeared, the makers of this printed shelf paper tried to keep it alive by switching from paper to plastic. But a change in the material did not help, as in the cities, closed cabinets began replacing open shelves, and the rural areas are following the lead of the cities. This "paper", now only in plastic, is still sold in the same shops where it was traditionally sold, but few people use it any more.

309   Corner of kitchen, showing shelf adorned with geometric-design paper

310   Printed paper lanterns form a simple street decoration

311   Paper doilies imitating embroidered or lace ones are still used in displaying pastries

229

glossary

Alpargata. Rope-soled sandal. Regional names include *esparteñas,* in Murcia; *espardenyes,* in Ibiza; and *espardenyas,* in Valencia. The latter all refer to the esparto used in making them.

Alpujarra. Mountainous region south of the Sierra Nevada, in the provinces of Granada and Almería.

Ampurdán. Region of the province of Gerona; its principal towns are Figueras and La Bisbal.

Belén. "Bethlehem", traditional Nativity scene, also called *pesebre* (manger) in Catalonia.

Bench. Wooden bench with back and sometimes with arms.

Blonde lace. Silk lace; originally of raw-silk color, hence the name.

Bone lace. Lace made using elongated, lathed bobbins of wood. Each of the various strands is wound around the upper, more slender part of a bobbin, while the lower, heavier end serves as a weight to hold the strand taut.

Botijo. A vessel for carrying and drinking water. It is most often made of unglazed, porous clay, so that slow transpiration and evaporation keep the water cool. To drink properly from a *botijo,* the drinker holds it up at arm's length and tilts the narrow spout down toward his open, up-turned mouth.

Cabezudo. One of the large cardboard heads worn by participants in certain festivals and processions.

Capazo. A large *espuerta* of reeds or wicker, used in the fields for agricultural products.

Castanets. Percussion instrument made of wood; it can be of various sizes, but is always worked by movement of the fingers or the palm of the hand. (From the Spanish *castañeta,* diminutive of *castaña,* chestnut. The more common Spanish name for castanets, *castañuelas,* is another diminutive form of the same word).

Ceramics. The origin of the term is Greek, and the term takes in objects of clay, china, and porcelain of all kinds and qualities.

Charro. Rural villager from the province of Salamanca.

Cinch. See girth.

Cofín. Flexible esparto basket which is filled with ground olives to crush them and extract the oil.

Cofradía. "Community" or "brotherhood", one of many lay religious organizations in the Catholic churches in Spain.

Crock. Clay vessel, glazed on the inside, which is used to keep small amounts of preserves.

Crupper. Wide strap attached to saddle or pack-saddle and looped under the animal's tail, to keep weight on its back from shifting. Sometimes it is even made of wood.

Cuévano. Large basket wider at the mouth than at the base, often meant to be carried on the back.

Enchinada. From *china,* little stone. Fine earthenware which is incrusted with small stones or pebbles while still soft.

Esparto. A kind of grass native to Spain and northern Africa, used in basketry and related crafts.

Espuerta. Flexible, concave-shaped basket, used to carry earth, manure, or agricultural products.

Fair. Larger-than-usual market which is held in a public place on specific days.

Farrapeiras. See *retaleras.*

Gazpacho. A cold soup made with bread, olive oil, vinagar, garlic, and vegetables.

Giant. In Spanish, *gigante;* very large papier mâché figure which appears in popular festivals and processions.

Girth. Hemp or sailcloth band tightened around body of animal to secure saddle or pack-saddle.

Horchata. Refreshing beverage very popular along the Levantine coast of Spain, made with crushed seeds (usually *chufa*, or groundnuts) and water.

Lamido. Technique of decorating pottery, in which a layer of clay paste is applied over the piece and designs made on this layer with a smooth stone which gives a patina to the surface it touches.

Levante. Southeastern part of Spain, on the Mediterranean coast.

Mantilla. Large veil covering woman's hair and shoulders. Diminutive of *manta,* mantle.

Masía. Typical rural house of Catalonia.

Osier. Species of willow used in wicker work.

Pack-saddle. Cushion placed on the back of a beast of burden, to bear the weight.

Palmetto. Kinds of small palm, especially dwarf fan-palm.

Palmón. Large palm branch, worked or unworked, carried to church for blessing on Palm Sunday. Augmentative of *palma,* palm.

Pepona. Large cardboard doll. Augmentative of Pepa, nickname for Josefa or Josefina.

Picador. In bullfight, man with lance mounted on horse which the bull must charge. From *picar,* to prick.

Porrón. Glass vessel with a long neck and a long, conical spout originating in the wide body, used for drinking wine. The technique for drinking is similar to that of the *botijo.*

Randa. From the German *Rand,* border. Trimming of lace or cloth which is placed at the edge of a piece of cloth or furniture.

Retaleras. Fabric made with warp of thread and woof of strips of cloth.

This is known by different names in different regions; *farrapeiras, mantarras, traperas, harapas.*

Romería. Popular festival at or pilgrimage to local hermitage or shrine, held on a village's religious holiday.

Siurells. Popular name given in Majorca to clay pipes or whistles, from *xiulet* (whistle).

Tinaja. Very large, wide-mouthed clay receptacle used for keeping water, wine, oil, or cereals.

Traperas. See *retaleras.*

Votive offering. Offering made in fulfillment of a vow, in gratitude for Divine assistance. It is usually a pictorial or sculptural representation of the favors bestowed.

Warp. Threads stretched lengthwise in loom to be crossed by woof.

Woof. Weft, cross-threads woven into warp.

index of places

bibliography

Amades, Joan, *Apunts d'Imatgeria,* Barcelona, 1938.

Amades, Joan, *El Pessebre,* Les Belles Edicions, Barcelona, 1946.

Amades, Joan, *Els Ex-vots,* Editorial Orbis, Barcelona, 1952.

Amades, Joan, *La Nina.* Private edition, Barcelona, 1965 (posthumous publication).

L'Art Popular Decoratiu a Catalunya, Barcelona, 1948.

Bossert Th., Helmuth, *Folk Art of Europe, Part I,* Frederick A. Praeger, New York, 1953.

Caro Baroja, Julio, *Los Pueblos de España,* Barcelona, 1946.

Casas, Joaquín, "Una Artesanía que Desaparece", *La Vanguardia,* Jan. 23, 1972.

Castells, F., "Títeres", Espasa-Calpe Supplement, 1971-72.

Comas, Rosa, and Jiménez Arqués, Inmaculada, "Tejidos Alpujarreños", *Narria* n° 3, Universidad Autónoma de Madrid, 1976.

Corredor-Matheos and Llorens Artigas, *Cerámica Popular Española,* Editorial Blume, Barcelona, 1974.

Ferré de Ruiz-Narváez, "Punta al Boixet", *Revista del F.A.D.,* Barcelona, May, 1928.

Gallardo, A. and Rubió y Tuduri, S., *La Farga Catalana,* Barcelona, 1930.

García Lorca, F., *Retablillo de Don Cristóbal. Farsa para guiñol,* 1931.

Giner de los Ríos, Hermenegildo, *Artes Industriales,* Ed. Antonio López, Barcelona.

González Hontoria, Guadalupe, *La Industria Artesana,* Madrid, 1969.

González Hontoria and Allende Salazar, *La Industria Artesana,* Ediciones de la Junta Central de Información, Turismo y Educación Popular, 1969.

González, Primitivo, "Alfarería", articles published in the newspaper *El Norte de Castilla,* December, 1976.

Hommage aux mains, Artisanat contemporain mondial. Exhibit catalog.

Hoyos Sainz, Luis, and Hoyos Sancho, Nieves de, *Manual de Folklore,* Madrid, 1947.

Jürgen Hansen, Hans, *Arte Popular Europeo,* prologue by L. Cortés Vázquez, Barcelona, 1969.

Krüger, Fritz, *El Mobiliario Popular en los Países Románicos,* Coimbra, 1963, and in monographic articles included in various specialized magazines.

Musée National des Arts et Traditions Populaires, *Arts Populaires Graphiques,* E. Musées Nationaux, Paris, 1974.

Museo del Pueblo Español, *Trabajos y Materiales.* Catalogs of the collections.

Nonell, C. "El Bordado Lagarterano", *Revista de las Artes y Oficios,* 1951, n° 77, pp. 17-19.

Pérez Bueno, L. *Vidrios y Vidrieras,* Barcelona, 1942.

Pérez Contel, R. *Trigo, Harina y Pan en Refranes,* Játiva, 1972.

Planell, L., *Vidrio, Historia, Tradición y Arte,* 2 volumenes, Barcelona, 1948.

Revista de Dialectología y Tradiciones Populares, "Panes Rituales, Infantiles y Juveniles, en el Nordeste y Levante Español", Madrid, 1958.

Rovirosa, Josep, "Las Puntaires", in the series, "Oficios" in the *Correo Catalán.*

Sánchez Queirolo, Augusto, "Las Puntaires de Arbós, una Reliquia Artesanal", in *La Vanguardia,* July 11, 1976.

Seseña, Natacha, *Barros y Lozas de España,* Editorial Prensa Española, Madrid 1976. A guide to potteries of Spain.

Soulier, Pierre, *Marionnettes, leur manipulation, leur théâtre,* Guide Ethnologique 17. Editions des Musées Nationaux.

Stapley, Mildred, *Tejidos y Bordados Populares Españoles,* Editorial Voluntad, S.A., Madrid, 1924.

Subias-Galter, J. *El Arte Popular en España,* Barcelona, 1948.

Useros, Carmina and Belmonte, Manuel, *En Busca de la Artesanía de Albacete,* Albacete, 1973.

"Comunicados al Congreso Internacional de las Artes Populares", report to the International Congress of Folk Arts, Prague, 1928.

Violant i Simorra, R. *El Arte Popular Español,* Aymá Editores, Barcelona, 1953.

Violant i Simorra, R., *La Indústria Casolana del Pa al Pallars Sobirà,* Barcelona, 1936.

spanish museums connected with the field of folk art

Avila
Museo de Arte Popular

Balearics Islands
Museo Regional, *Artá*
Museo Arqueológico, *Ibiza*
Museo de Bellas Artes, *Mahón*
Museo de Mallorca, Ethnology Section, *Muró*
Museo Etnico, *San Antonio Abad*

Barcelona
Museo Etnológico
Museo de Artes Decorativas y Legado Cambó
Museo de la Indumentaria, *Rocamora*
Museo Local, *Cardedeu*
Museo de la Ciudad, *Sabadell*
Museo del Cau Ferrat, *Sitges*

Museo de Maricel, *Sitges*
Museo Textil Biosca, *Tarrasa*

Bilbao
Museo Arqueológico de Vizcaya y Etnográfico Vasco

Burgos
Museo de Ricas Telas

Cáceres
Museo Provincial de Bellas Artes

Cádiz
Museo de Bellas Artes

Córdoba
Museo Provincial de Bellas Artes
Museo Taurino y de Artesanía

Gerona
Museo Folklórico, *Ripoll*

Las Palmas de Gran Canaria
Museo Canario

Pamplona
Museo Etnográfico del Pirineo

Santander
Museo Etnográfico, *Muriedas*

Sevilla
Museo de Artes y Costumbres Populares

Toledo
Museo de Artes Aplicadas Toledanas